WILD FLOWERS
AND WHERE TO FIND THEM
IN NORTHERN ENGLAND

VOLUME TWO

Waterside Ways

WILD FLOWERS
AND WHERE TO FIND THEM
IN NORTHERN ENGLAND

VOLUME TWO

Waterside Ways

LAURIE FALLOWS

FRANCES LINCOLN

A pocket guide to the wild flowers of Northern England, their historical, folk-mythological and medicinal attributes, with some background essays on related topics ❀ When and where to find them, their identifying features and flowering periods ❀ Detailed self-guided walks with simple maps to facilitate discovery

Volume 2
Waterside Ways
Streamsides, pond margins, bog and coastal areas

Also in this series
Volume 1
Northern Limestone
Limestone meadows, pastures and woods

Volume 3
Acid Uplands
Mountain, moorland and acid heaths

Frances Lincoln Ltd
4 Torriano Mews
Torriano Avenue
London NW5 2RZ
www.franceslincoln.com

© 2004 Laurie Fallows
Edited and designed by Jane Havell

ISBN 0 7112 2029 8

Origination by Imagescan, Malaysia
Printed in China by C S Graphics

Half-title page: (top) Burnet Rose; (centre) Tufted Vetch; (bottom) Forget-me-not
Title pages: Buttercup and Ragged Robin in a wet meadow

09921932

CONTENTS

Acknowledgements

I would like to express my heartfelt thanks to my wife Hazel, for her patience, support and understanding; to my daughter Jane and grandson Andrew for their invaluable assistance in the hitherto dark realms of computer wizardry; to my other daughter Gay and friend Joyce Langtree for assistance with fieldwork and walk-planning.

I would like to dedicate these three volumes to my late mother Mary, née Vickers, for stimulating my initial interest in the flowers that played such an important part in her life, especially in her native Corbridge on Tyne, Northumberland.

LF
Windermere
2003

INTRODUCTION

For over fifty years I have conducted guided walks for National Park and local government authorities, and for educational and recreational organisations in the Yorkshire Dales, the Lake District, the Cheviots, the Galloway Hills of southern Scotland, and Snowdonia. I have introduced many thousands of adults and occasionally schoolchildren to the countryside, stressing not only the physical enjoyment of the great outdoors but also an understanding of its scenery, its history and its wildlife.

The information most frequently requested concerned the identification, the habitats, the folklore, the culinary and medicinal uses of plants, and simple field guides to help with their recognition. As more and more people take quiet recreation in country walks, the need for simple, descriptive, illustrated guides to wild flowers has increased. Existing flower guides have a number of drawbacks for beginners. They often rely on a knowledge of botanical terms, and do not indicate where particular species may be found. Furthermore, most of those that give flowering periods relate to central and southern England, whereas in the north of the country the climate, altitude and latitude often delay flowering by several weeks.

The plants covered in these books are of course not specific to the region, but can be found in other regions with similar soils and climates throughout the rest of Britain and Europe, making these guides of universal value.

Descriptions are stated in the simplest terms, and do not require any knowledge of the technical vocabulary of botanists. Read in association with the colour photographs, they should prevent confusion and make for certain identification. The flowering charts are based on regular personal observation throughout the year, and should provide an accurate record of when to see the plants in flower in northern England.

The walks are located in the Lake District and Southern Lakeland, the Yorkshire Dales, and Upper Teesdale. The straightforward instructions are

Low Force, Bowlees, Teesdale

illustrated by specially drawn, simple maps, with a note of the relevant Ordnance Survey maps for those who want further cartographical information. Distances are given in kilometres, miles and average times. While some of the walks are longer than others, the maps often show how they may be shortened. Occasionally, fairly steep gradients and rough or boggy terrain will be encountered – where appropriate, these factors are mentioned.

RESPECT FOR HABITATS

All the plants featured in this book have been recorded within two metres of public or permissive footpaths. If the walk guides are followed, there is no risk of trespass. Remember to tread carefully and avoid trampling plants when looking at or photographing them, especially rare species.

Plants must never be picked or uprooted. Apart from being illegal (see box, page 9), removing them detracts from the natural environment.

WILD PLANTS AND THE LAW

All plants growing in the wild and their habitats are protected by the Wildlife and Countryside Act, 1981. Section 13 states: 'It is an offence for anyone to intentionally pick, uproot or destroy any wild plant on schedule 8,' which includes, among others, Spring Gentians, Bluebells, Pennyroyal, Teesdale Sandwort, Slender Naiad and some ferns, lichens and mosses. European legislation embodied in Conservation (Natural Habitats, etc.) Regulations 1994 adds further plants including Lady's Slipper Orchid, Shore Dock and Yellow Marsh Saxifrage. Section 13 (1)(b) of the 1981 Act states: 'it is an offence for any unauthorised person to intentionally uproot *any* wild plant,' – i.e., whether it is protected or not. Dealing in wild plants is forbidden under Section13 (2) (9a), which makes it an offence to 'sell, offer or expose for sale or possess or transport for the purpose of sale, or advertisement of intent to sell, any live or dead wild plant (or any part of or anything derived from such a plant) on schedule 8.'

Section 4 (3) of the Theft Act 1968 states that the picking of wild flowers, fruit or fungi for reward is considered to be theft. Uprooting a whole plant may also be considered theft. In Scotland, damage to flowers or plants on someone's property may be punishable as vandalism under the Criminal Law (Consolidation) (Scotland) Act 1995, Section 52, or as the common law crime of malicious mischief.

CONSUMPTION

The herbal uses described in this guide are for general interest only. Plants and plant extracts must not be applied to the skin or taken internally without reference to a qualified herbalist or at least an up-to-date herbal. Very careful identification is essential before any kind of experiment. Even in recent times, people have died through incorrect identification of plants – for example, by confusing Foxglove leaves with Comfrey. Identification should be by examining the whole plant, not just the flower or the leaf alone, since there are many superficial similarities.

HOW TO USE THE FLOWER DIRECTORY

The plants are grouped according to the main colours of their flowers. However, many may be present in different colours – for example, Mountain Pansies are normally yellow in the Dales, but more likely to be blue or purple in Teesdale; Milkwort varies from blue or pink to white. Flower colour should be only one factor in identifying a species.

CHARTS

The Directory is preceded by colour charts, showing the months in which the plants may be seen in flower in northern England. Colours can vary considerably, even within species, so this should be taken as only a rough guide to aid identification. For simplification, and because colour is often subjective, the charts include some flowers that fit only marginally into the given colour categories.

While the charts are a general guide to flowering times in Northern England, individual specimens may flower outside these months. This may be because of peculiar local conditions, or because some species flower in profusion for a month or two and then produce a second flush later in the year. Groundsel, Chickweed and Red Campion may be seen virtually all the year round.

The charts are original, and have been compiled over six years by personal observation throughout the year. Flowering times may therefore vary from those published in other guides, many of which describe lower latitudes and altitudes. However, the region does range from the mild, moist southern Lakeland through the drier and higher Yorkshire Dales to the wet high altitude of Upper Teesdale, so variation is inevitable.

PHOTOGRAPHS

Each species is illustrated by a colour photograph, showing the general appearance of the plant, and the shape and relative size of its leaves and flowers. Please note that the scale of the individual photographs is not consistent.

NAMES

The main regional vernacular name is given first, then any other names in common use. Where there are many alternative names, only a selection is given. Vernacular names can be confusing. In different parts of the country, a single flower can have many different names – Cuckoo Pint, for example, has at least ninety recorded local names. The name Thunderflower is used for both Wood Anemone and Wood Cranesbill; Aaron's Rod for Agrimony and Great Mullein. The Bluebell of England becomes the Hyacinth in parts of Scotland, and their Bluebell is the English Harebell. Latin names are therefore also given to aid precise identification. Wherever possible, the origin and explanation of both Latin and common names are also expounded.

ABBREVIATIONS

aka	also known as
Arab	Arabic
AS	Anglo-Saxon
Celt	Celtic
Fr	French
Ger	German
Gk	Greek
L	Latin
ODan	Old Danish
OE	Old English
OFr	Old French
ON	Old Norse

HEIGHT AND FLOWERING MONTHS

When identifying a plant do not refer just to the photograph, but also to the height in the written description.

DESCRIPTION

The first paragraph describes general characteristics. The second paragraph gives particulars of where the plant grows, and an indication of its place in folklore and in folk and contemporary medicine.

IDENTIFICATION TIPS

When trying to identify a plant you do not know, it is important to consider all its features – particularly the shape of both flower and leaves, whether or

BOTANICAL TERMS

Every effort has been made to keep plant descriptions as simple as possible, but a few botanical terms are unavoidable.

alternate arranged alternately up the stem

annual completing a full life cycle in one year

anthers cases on top of stamens that contain pollen

basal just above ground level at the foot of the stem

biennial forming a rosette of basal leaves the first year; raising a stem, flowering and dying in the second year

bract small, leaf-like organ on flower stem

calyx sepals at flower base, often joined in a cup or tube

deciduous shedding leaves in the autumn

floret individual flower in a tight arrangement, as in Daisy

labiate in two parts, like lips

lanceolate lance-shaped

leaflet one division of a compound leaf

lobed divided into sections

node place on stem where leaves arise

ovary the seed container below the style

perennial going on year after year with incremental vegetative increase

persistent leaves overwinter on plant

petals inner leaves, often highly coloured, of flower heads

pinnate divided into leaflets either side of stalk

raceme flower spike

rhizome swollen underground root that feeds the plant

sepals outer leaves of flower buds and holders of flower

stamens male pollen-bearing organs

stigma top of the style that receives the pollen

stipules small leaf-like appendages at the base of leaf stalks

stolons creeping stems that produce new plant stems at intervals

style tube or stalk between stigma and ovary

trefoil with three leaflets, as in Clover

tubers swollen underground organs with plant food

wintergreen retaining old leaves over winter

not parts are hairy, whether it is growing in dry or wet conditions, in sun or in shade, and whether it is shunned or devoured by livestock. Consider its situation in relation to the type of ground it is growing in and its association with other plant life. Climate and altitude can also cause considerable variation. The walks section gives further information about when and where to locate certain species.

A small hand lens of 10× magnification is very helpful in identification, and also reveals the hidden beauties of diminutive species.

THE NAMING OF FLOWERS

'What's in a name? That which we call a rose
By any other name would smell as sweet'
Shakespeare, *Romeo and Juliet* (II, ii)

Consider these local flower names:

Bachelor's Buttons, Bee's Rest, Big Buttercup, Billy Buttons, Blogda, Blugga, Bobby's Buttons, Dog Daisy, Boots, Bull Buttercup, Bull Cup, Bulldogs, Bull Flower, Bull Rushes, Bull's Eyes, Butterbleb, Buttercup, Butter Flower, Carlicaps, Chims, Clant, Cow Lily, Cow Cranes, Cowslops, Crazy, Crazy Bets, Crazy Betsy, Crazy Betty, Crazy Lilies, Crow Cranes, Crow Flower, Cup and Saucer, Dale Cup, Downscwobs, Drunkan, Fiddle, Fire o' Gold, Giloup, Gypsys, Money, Gilty Cup, Golden Cup, Golden Knob, Golden Kingcup, Goldicup, Goldilocks, Golland, Gowan, Grandfather's Buttons, Halcup, Horse Blob, Horse Hooves, Horse Buttercup, John Georges, Johnny Cranes, King's Cob, Kingcup, Livers, Mare Blobs, Marigold, Marsh Lily, Marybout, Marybuds, Mary's Gold, May Blob, May Blubs, May Bubbles, May Flower, Meadowbout, Meadowbright, Moll Blob, Molly Blob, Monkey Bells, Old Man's Buttons, Policeman's Buttons, Publicans, Soldier's Buttons, Water Babies, Water Blebs, Water Blobs, Water Blubbers, Water Buttercup, Water Geordies, Water Goggles, Water Golland, Water Gowland, Water Gowan, Waterlily, Wildfire, Yellow Blobs, Yellow Boots, Yellow Crazies, Yellow Gowlan.

Each of these 93 different names is applied in different localities to the 94th and more common MARSH MARIGOLD.

Consider also the following flowers that in various places are called BACHELOR'S BUTTONS:

Buttercup, Burdock, Red Campion, White Campion, Cornflower, Shining Cranesbill, Columbine, Devil's Bit Scabious, Field Scabious, Feverfew, Herb Robert, Knapweed, Marsh Marigold, Navelwort, Pennywort, Periwinkle, Ragged Robin, Sneezewort, Greater Stitchwort, Tansy and Yellow Water Lily

or those locally named CUCKOO FLOWER:

Wood Anemone, Red Campion, White Campion, Cuckoo Pint, Greater Stitchwort, Bluebell, Meadow Saxifrage, Wood Sorrel, Marsh Violet, Early Purple Orchid, Marsh Orchid and Green Winged Orchid.

These delightfully evocative vernacular names were too imprecise for the scholars and physicians who practised botany and healing in times when medicine was almost wholly based on the perceived properties of plants (for more detail, see Volume 1, *Northern Limestone*). From records preserved in monasteries and the burgeoning universities, we know that by the Middle Ages Greek, Latin and Arabic names were also in common currency. The commonest names were Latin, no longer the language of classical times but rather one adapted by individuals to meet their personal perceptions of plants. Often there were no appropriate Latin words for newly discovered species or their parts and descriptions, so a new vocabulary, loosely based on classical Latin, was gradually introduced to make identification easier and more precise.

Known as Botanical Latin, it had a parallel in the Dog Latin used by the medieval church. In 1923 R. A. Knox wrote: 'a proverb tells us that a living dog is better than a dead lion, and the difference between the Dog Latin of St Jerome and the Lion Latin of Cicero is the difference between a living and a dead language.' This is also true of Botanical Latin. Scholars, doctors, scientists and botanists in many nations aimed over the years to standardise and codify the language they used in their studies.

The Swedish doctor and botanist Carl Linnaeus (1707–78) developed a universally accepted system by which all plants and animals could be named,

A bank of Forget-me-not (*Myosotis arvensis*; page 94)

classified and described. He assigned to each plant a family name (*genus*, plural *genera*) and within that an individual or specific name (*species*). These two elements make up the scientific names of plants. The genus is always written with an initial capital and the species in lower case – as in *Ranunculus repens* (the Buttercup that creeps). Occasionally, cross-fertilisation produces unusual plants, and the symbol × is used to indicate the cross. Thus the False Oxlip, a cross between the Cowslip (*Primula veris*) and the Primrose (*Primula vulgaris*), is represented as *Primula veris × vulgaris*; the Yellow Water Avens, a cross between the normally creamy pink Water Avens (*Geum rivale*) and the yellow Herb Bennet (*Geum urbanum*) is designated as *Geum rivale × urbanum*.

White Butterbur (*Petasites albus*; page 54) by the River Wharfe

This so-called binomial system was quickly adopted by botanists and doctors throughout the world, replacing the cumbersome and imprecise procedure of naming plants by referring to their characteristics. This nomenclature has allowed people of all countries and languages to name plants with a certainty that cannot be misunderstood, whatever the plants' local names.

Linnaeus used Latin names where they were in common use, including the Latinisation of some Greek or Arabic names. Where no satisfactory name existed he, and others after him, created new names for genera. These might refer to the plant's discoverer, as in *Linnaea* (after Linnaeus) and *Minuartia* (after Juan Minuart of Barcelona, 1693–1768); its physical features, as in *Polygonum* (many knees) and *Conopodium* (cone-footed); the place where it grew, as in *Convallaria* (from the valleys) and *Parnassia* (of Parnassus), or the ailment it was thought to cure, as in *Scrophularia* (from the swelling of neck glands) and *Pulmonaria* (from lung infections).

Linnaeus also attempted to standardise the naming of the parts of plants. He did this by simplifying existing names, Latinising them where possible according to his system of classification, and stipulating guidelines for the naming of new discoveries.

Linnaeus's classification was a refinement of earlier attempts by Englishman John Ray (1628–1705) and Frenchman Joseph Pitton de Tournefort (1656–1708). It was based on the shape and function of the plants' reproductive organs. Twenty separate groups of plants with stamens and pistils in the same flower; a further three with stamens and pistils in different flowers, and a last group without flowers (such as mosses) made up the principal 24 classes.

The classes were given the suffixes *-andrias* (Gk male), *-oecias* (Gk room) and *-gamias* (Gk united). These classes were subdivided into orders, based on the plants' female characteristics, their styles and stigmas. These were named *Monogynia*, *Digynia*, *Trigynia* and so forth (Gk *gyna*, female).

Linnaeus's relatively youthful and ingenuous obsession with the genital organs of plants both scandalised a puritanical public and drew ridicule from some contemporaries. Even as late as 1808, Rev. Samuel Goodenough, later to become Bishop of Carlisle, wrote: 'A literal translation of the first principles of Linnaean botany is enough to shock female modesty. It is possible that many virtuous students might not be able to make out the similitude of *Clitoria*.' And in 1820, Goethe expressed concern that the chaste souls of women and young people should not be embarrassed by botanical textbooks expounding the 'dogma of sexuality'. Erasmus Darwin, grandfather of Charles, lampooned the Linnaean system, referring to stamens as knights, husbands, brothers and youths, and pistils as nymphs, wives and virgins. Other respectable botanists were equally derisive.

The rather fanciful classification, while popular for a few decades spanning the death of Linnaeus, was eventually replaced by a system based on John Ray's. But the introduction of Latin binomial nomenclature was Linnaeus's lasting memorial. It made botany accessible to professional and amateur students all over the world at a time of rapidly widening geographical horizons and an explosion in botanical exploration during the eighteenth century.

GEOLOGY OF THE REGION

In Volume 1, *Northern Limestone*, the earth's structure and the rocks that cover its surface were briefly described. Here I shall look at the results of erosion by water and weather, and the deposition of sediments that cloak the underlying rocks and offer different surface soils and habitats.

ALLUVIUM AND GLACIAL DRIFT

The newer rocks on the earth's surface, whether of sedimentary or volcanic origin, have not been consolidated by undue heat or pressure and are therefore more susceptible to the erosive effects of rain, running water, moving ice, frost-shattering and wind. The tiny fragments of silt, sand or fine gravel loosened from base rocks by these actions are carried along by surface water, always flowing gravitationally downwards. In the broader, less steep, lower reaches of a river or glacier, decreasing water current allows the grains to settle and build up into an ever-deepening mantle of alluvium that spreads across the flood zone of the valley floor. Originating from a wide spectrum of rock sources along the river's catchment area, it contains a mixture of elements from lime-rich to acid, and can often support a great variety of plants. These broad, flat areas have been much exploited by farmers, although many have had to be drained to overcome waterlogging.

Similar processes were followed by the more violent glaciers of the Ice Ages which, in addition to valley bottom deposition, heaped up their debris in reasonably well-drained, often lime-rich, moraines and drumlins.

WATER MARGINS

Erosion is never complete. Enhanced by spates, often arrested by drought, river banks and river beds are constantly changing, with former embankments and ox-bow lakes indicating earlier courses. Lakes and tarns, continu-

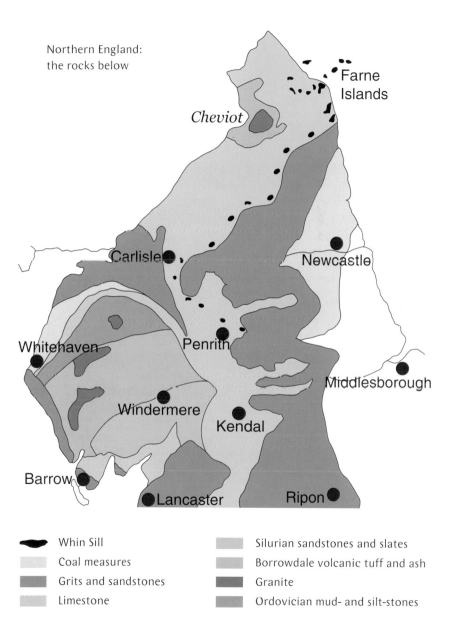

Northern England:
the rocks below

Farne
Islands

Cheviot

Carlisle

Newcastle

Whitehaven

Penrith

Middlesborough

Windermere

Kendal

Barrow

Lancaster

Ripon

	Whin Sill		Silurian sandstones and slates
	Coal measures		Borrowdale volcanic tuff and ash
	Grits and sandstones		Granite
	Limestone		Ordovician mud- and silt-stones

GEOLOGICAL TIME CHART

Period	million yrs ago	Location	Origin
Carboniferous			
Whin Sill	295	Under N Pennines	Volcanic
Millstone Grit	300	Central Pennines	Deltaic
Coal Measures	310	W Cumberland, Durham and Northumberland	Swamp
Yoredale Series		Yorkshire Dales	Cyclic deposition
Great Limestone	345	S and E of Lakes	Marine skeletons
Caledonian Uplift	410	Lakes and Pennines	Volcanic
Silurian	450	South Lakes	Deep ocean silt
Borrowdale Volcanics	460	Central Lakes	Volcanic
Ordovician	510	North Lakes	Deep sea mud

ously fed with the detritus of feeder becks or streams, are forever silting up, causing natural shrinkage that is arrested only temporarily by flooding. Plants growing on river banks and lake shores are under constant attack from different conditions, and therefore need to be very resilient to survive. Nevertheless, river and beck sides, and the edges of lakes and tarns, support a wide range of plants that can tolerate all the vicissitudes of torrent, submersion, freezing, ice, waterlogging, drought, animal trampling and grazing – and, now, the unnatural threats of agricultural chemicals.

SALT MARSHES

Beyond the mainland, inter-tidal salt marshes are colonised by unique plant species that can withstand both regular inundation by the sea and buffeting by waves and wind, and the high salinity of the muds and sands in which they spread their roots. Many have specialised mechanisms. Sea Lavender (*Limonium* species) excretes salt through glands in its leaves; the succulent Glasswort (*Salicornia europaea*) can tolerate high levels of salt by diluting it with its own inbuilt water content. Ultimately, unless swept away by storms, salt marshes build up their own colonies of plants that eventually raise the surface above the influence of the tide; they then are regraded as reed

Sea Holly (*Eryngium maritimum*; page 940) on Walney Island dunes

swamps. These in turn will dry out and be slowly colonised by encroaching grasses and herbs, causing a further regrading as pasture or copse. Further details of these processes are exemplified more specifically in the introduction to the Walks section featuring Walney Island (page 108).

Overleaf: Marsh Ragwort (*Senecio aquaticus*; page 43) at Loup Scar by the River Wharfe

FLOWER DIRECTORY

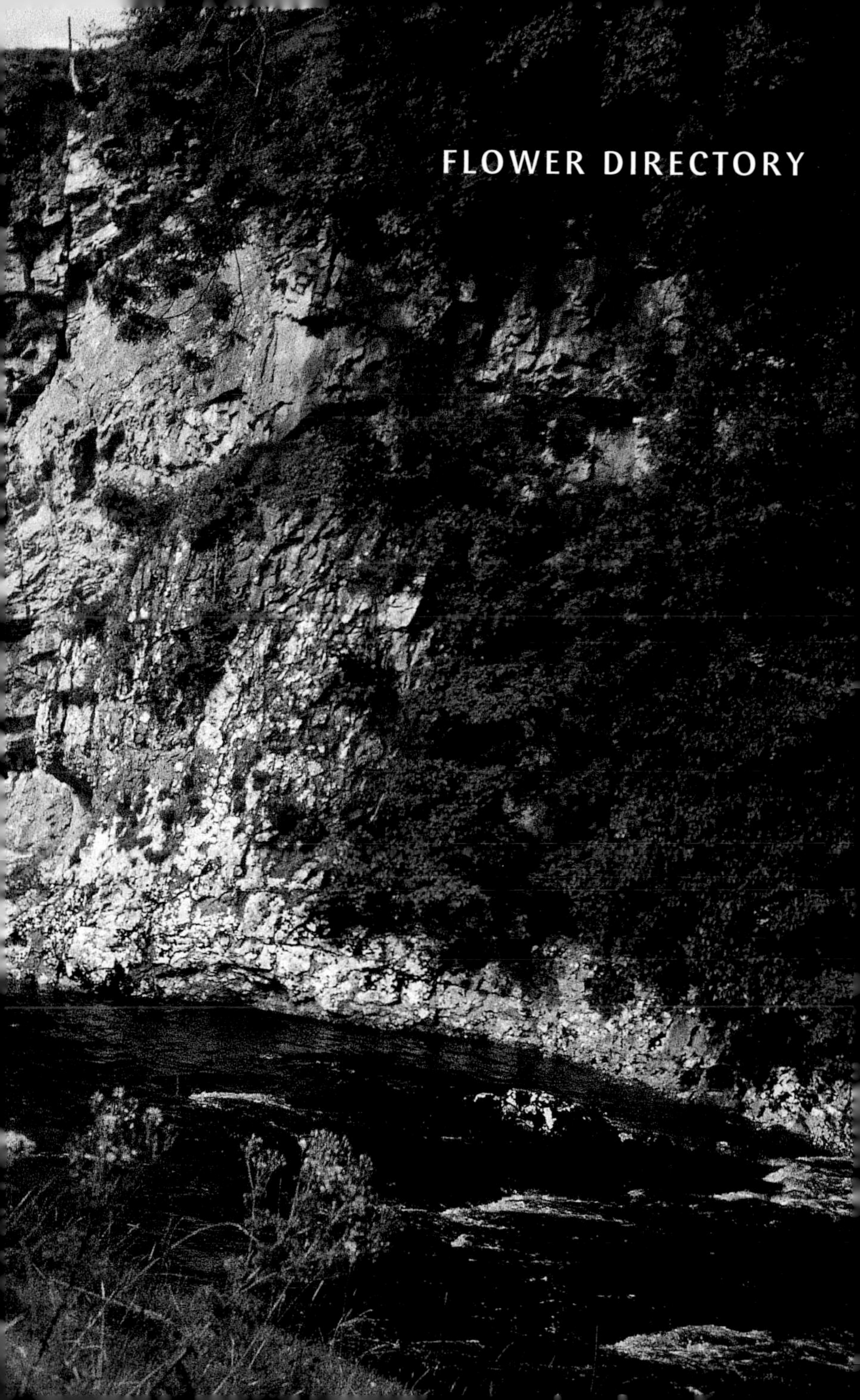

PLANTS IN FLOWER	Jan	Feb	Mar	Apr	May	June	July	Aug	Sep	Oct	Nov	Dec
Balsam, Small												
Buttercup, Creeping												
Buttercup, Goldilocks												
Buttercup, Meadow												
Coltsfoot												
Cudweed, Marsh												
Dyer's Greenweed												
Flag, Yellow												
Fox and Cubs												
Glasswort												
Goatsbeard												
Groundsel												
Groundsel, Sticky												
Hawkbit, Autumnal												
Hawkbit, Rough												
Hawksbeard, Marsh												
Hawksbeard, Smooth												
Henbane												
Lady's Mantle, Smooth												
Lady's Mantle, Yellow-Green												
Loosestrife, Yellow												
Lupin, Tree												
Marigold, Marsh												
Mayweed, Pineapple												
Monkey Flower												
Mugwort												
Nipplewort												
Poppy, Welsh												
Poppy, Yellow Horned												
Primrose, Evening												
Purslane, Sea												
Ragwort, Marsh												
Ragwort, Oxford												
Rattle, Yellow												
Sow Thistle, Smooth												
St John's Wort, Slender												
Tansy												
Toadflax												
Touch-Me-Not												
Trefoil, Hop												
Vetch, Kidney												
Vetchling, Meadow												
Water Lily, Yellow												
Weld												
Wintercress												

PLANTS IN FLOWER	Jan	Feb	Mar	Apr	May	June	July	Aug	Sep	Oct	Nov	Dec
Bindweed, Great												
Bindweed, Hedge												
Bittercress, Hairy												
Bittercress, Variant												
Bittercress, Wavy												
Bramble												
Bramble, Stone												
Butterbur, White												
Campion, Bladder												
Campion, Sea												
Chickweed												
Clover, White												
Deadnettle, White												
Dewberry												
Elder												
Elder, Ground												
Feverfew												
Fool's Watercress												
Gipsywort												
Helleborine, Marsh												
Hogweed												
Hogweed, Giant												
Kale, Sea												
Knotgrass												
Mayweed, Sea												
Mouse-Ear												
Mouse-Ear, Sticky												
Nightshade, Black												
Parsley, Cow												
Rockcress, Hairy												
Rose, Burnet												
Rose, Field												
Sandwort, Sea												
Saxifrage, Meadow												
Shepherd's Purse												
Stitchwort, Greater												
Violet, Dame's												
Water Crowfoot, Pond												
Water Dropwort, Hemlock												
Water Lily, White												
Watercress												
Wintergreen, Round-Leaved												

PLANTS IN FLOWER	Jan	Feb	Mar	Apr	May	June	July	Aug	Sep	Oct	Nov	Dec
Aster, Sea							■	■	■	■		
Comfrey					■	■	■	■	■			
Figwort						■	■	■				
Fumitory					■	■	■	■				
Heartsease				■	■	■	■	■				
Hemp-Nettle							■	■				
Hound's Tongue						■	■					
Lavender, Sea							■	■				
Loosestrife, Purple						■	■	■				
Marjoram							■	■	■			
Milkwort, Sea					■	■	■	■	■			
Mint, Water							■	■	■			
Nightshade, Woody						■	■	■	■			
Rocket, Sea						■	■	■				
Vetch						■	■	■				
Vetch, Bitter				■	■	■						
Vetch, Bush				■	■	■	■	■	■			
Vetch, Tufted						■	■	■				
Woundwort, Hedge						■	■	■	■			

PLANTS IN FLOWER	Jan	Feb	Mar	Apr	May	June	July	Aug	Sep	Oct	Nov	Dec
Balsam, Himalayan							■	■	■			
Bindweed, Sea						■	■	■				
Geranium, Walney						■	■	■				
Mallow						■	■	■	■			
Mint, Spear-							■	■	■	■		
Orchid, Bee						■	■					
Purslane, Pink					■	■	■	■				
Rest Harrow						■	■	■	■			
Rose, Dog						■	■					
Scurvygrass, Danish				■	■	■	■	■				
Spurrey, Greater Sand-						■	■	■				
Storksbill					■	■	■	■				
Thrift				■	■	■	■	■				
Willowherb, Broad-Leaved						■	■	■	■	■		
Willowherb, Great							■	■	■			

PLANTS IN FLOWER	Jan	Feb	Mar	Apr	May	June	July	Aug	Sep	Oct	Nov	Dec
Campion, Red					■	■	■	■	■	■	■	
Clover, Red					■	■	■	■	■			
Deadnettle, Red			■	■								■
Pimpernel, Scarlet						■	■	■	■	■		

PLANTS IN FLOWER	Jan	Feb	Mar	Apr	May	June	July	Aug	Sep	Oct	Nov	Dec
Alkanet, Green					■	■	■	■	■			
Bugloss				■	■				■			
Bugloss, Viper's					■	■	■	■	■			
Cranesbill, Meadow						■	■	■	■			
Forget-Me-Not				■	■	■	■	■	■	■	■	
Holly, Sea						■	■	■	■			
Scabious, Field							■	■	■			
Sow-Thistle, Blue							■	■	■			
Speedwell, Thyme Leaved				■	■	■	■	■				

PLANTS IN FLOWER	Jan	Feb	Mar	Apr	May	June	July	Aug	Sep	Oct	Nov	Dec
Beet, Sea						■	■	■	■			
Bryony, Black					■	■	■	■				
Dock, Broad						■	■	■				
Good King Henry					■	■	■	■				
Naiad, Slender							■	■				
Pearlwort, Mossy					■	■	■	■				
Pondweed, Bog						■	■	■				
Saltwort							■	■	■			
Sorrel					■	■	■	■				
Spurge, Portland				■	■	■	■	■	■			
Spurge, Sea						■	■	■	■			
Town Hall Clock				■	■							

BALSAM, SMALL

Height 15–60cm/6–24in ❀ April–August

Impatiens parviflora
L *impatiens*, explosive; *parviflora*, puny flower

A weedy-looking annual with smooth, spindly, often reddish stems swollen at joints. Leaves toothed and pointed. Small yellow flowers resembling policemen's helmets on a slender stalk, unspotted and with a short straightish spur. Fruits borne in a slim club-shaped capsule that explodes when ripe. A nineteenth-century introduction from Russia that quickly naturalised in moist wooded or shaded places. Particularly prominent around Lake Windermere.

BUTTERCUP, CREEPING

Height 5–53cm/2–20in ❀ May–September

Ranunculus repens
L *rana*, frog (lives in damp places); *repens*, creeping

A perennial buttercup that roots from creeping runners. Long-stalked lower leaves divided into 3 lobes, deeply toothed, the middle one stalked, all leaves hairy. Flowers borne singly or in clusters, sepals erect, a waxy golden-yellow. Fruits a globular cluster of smooth green pear-shaped seeds. A common pest of heavy wet soils that rapidly multiplies by runners. Shunned by cattle since probably slightly poisonous.

Used as an ointment for skin troubles, bruises, sores, insect bites and 'kennels' (eye ulcers); bandaged to rheumatic joints it drew out the rheumatism in skin blisters! Once called 'Crazies' because the smell is alleged to cause insanity.

BUTTERCUP, GOLDILOCKS

WOOD BUTTERCUP, WOOD GOLDILOCKS,
CROWFOOT

Height 20–40cm/8–16in ❀ April–June

Ranunculus auricomus
L *rana*, frog; *auri*, little ear

A perennial buttercup with deeply lobed,
kidney-shaped, stalked basal leaves, slightly
hairy. Round hairy stalks have deeply divided
stem leaves with lance-shaped leaflets. Shiny
yellow flowers often imperfect, sometimes
with no petals or misshapen ones. Sepals
tipped purple. Downy fruits held in a tight
globular cluster. Common in lowland woods
and hedges.

Culpeper says: 'in no way to be given
inwardly, but an ointment of leaves or flowers
will draw a blister, and may be so fitly applied
to the nape of the neck to draw black rheum
from the eyes.'

BUTTERCUP, MEADOW

KINGCUP, CROWPECKLE, GOLDWEED,
SOLDIERS' BUTTONS, BUTTERFLOWER,
CROWFOOT

Height 30–90cm/12–36in ❀ May–October

Ranunculis acris
L *rana*, frog; *acris*, sharp taste

A hairy perennial of damp rich grassland
(calcareous soils). Individual plants; no
runners. Erect, usually hairy, little-branched
stems bear deeply cut palmate leaves in 3–7
narrow unstalked segments, toothed or lobed.
Stem leaves similar but smaller. Bright yellow
to white flowers have 5 erect sepals that
spread out as flowers open but do not bend
back. 5 petals. Unfurrowed flower stalks. Fruits
in round cluster, each with short hooked beak.

Poisonous. Medical uses doubtful, but roots
ground up with salt, applied to the skin, were
believed to draw out the plague. Flowers hung
round the neck were believed to cure lunacy.

COLTSFOOT

COUGHWORT, COLDWORT, CLEATS, FOAL-
FOOT, HORSE HOOF, ASS'S FOOT, BULL FOOT

Height 3–17cm/1¹/₂–7in ❀ February–April

Tussilago farfara
L *Tussilago*, plant name from *tussis*, cough

A perennial rising from an underground
rhizome; flowers before leaves. Yellow daisy-
like flowers borne on erect, purplish, scaly
stem. After flowering, mealy white heart-
shaped basal leaves with crinkled edges
appear. Umbrella-type leaves, upper parts
shiny, felted white below.

The apothecary's shop sign. As a tea or
candy, it was used for coughs and colds,
asthma, pleurisy, bites, ulcers, swellings and
burns. Dried leaves used as snuff and tobacco,
especially for asthmatics. Leaves dipped in
saltpetre used as tinder. Down from leaves and
seed heads made into soft pillows. Wine from
it called Clayt, beer Cleats. Young leaves, buds
and flowers give an aromatic flavour to salads.

CUDWEED, MARSH

WAYSIDE CUDWEED, COTTON-WEED,
MARCH EVERLASTING

Height 4–20cm/1¹/₂–8in ❀ July–August

Gnaphalium uliginosum
Gk *gnaphalium*, woolly; L *uliginosum*,
of marshland

A weak, many-branched, greyish annual.
Woolly hair covers stem and alternate slender,
lance-shaped leaves. Terminal flower heads
cradled in rosettes of leaves, consist of 3–10
dense clusters of short-stalked, rayless,
browny-yellow florets. Minute brown seeds. A
common insignificant plant of damp, lowland,
well-trodden tracks and waysides.

Astringent; used medicinally usually as a
gargle to treat quinsy and throat infection or
inflammation.

DYER'S GREENWEED

DYER'S BROOM, SHE-BROOM, WOADMESH

Height 30–70cm/12–28in ❀ July–September

Genista tinctoria
L *genista*, name of a small bush; *tinctoria*, dye

A perennial deciduous sub-shrub like a small
Broom. Branched erect stems bear downy-
edged, alternate, lance-shaped leaves. Yellow
pea-flowers borne in spikes on the tops with
standards the same size as keels. Fruits carried
in long pods that twist to disperse seeds when
ripe.

Widely grown by immigrant Flemish
weavers in damp places near Kendal. After
drying, boiled in water to produce a yellow
liquid. Woollen cloth boiled in alum water
was immersed into this to dye it yellow. When
dry it was soaked in blue dye from woad or
elderberries to produce the famous Kendal
Green cloth (Shakespeare, *Henry IV Part I*).

FLAG, YELLOW

YELLOW IRIS, MEKKINS, DRAGON FLOWER,
FLEUR DE LYS

Height 40–152cm/16–60in ❀ June–August

Iris pseudacoris
Gk *Iris*, goddess of the rainbow; L *pseudacoris*,
false acoris (a different flag)

A stout perennial with an underground
horizontal tuber. Its stiff broad sword-shaped
leaves have a raised midriff and parallel veins.
Strong round stems bear successions of large
yellow flowers with broad oval falls and erect
standards. Large erect seed pods contain many
brown seeds that float for dispersal. Common
in damp lowland places.

Poisonous when raw, so other species are
preferred medicinally. Thought to avert evil –
hung over Irish doors on Corpus Christi,
French doors on St John's Eve. Roasted seeds
once made into coffee. Rhizomes yield a black
dye and ink.

FOX AND CUBS

ORANGE HAWKWEED, GRIM THE COLLIER,
DEVIL'S PAINTBRUSH

Height 15–30cm/6–12in ✿ June–September

Hieracium aurantium
Gk *Hieracium*, plant name; L *aurantium*,
orange

A very hairy perennial with creeping roots
throwing up many flowering stems. Rosettes
of bluish-green, untoothed, lance-shaped
leaves are covered with dark hairs. Roughly
hairy erect stems bear crowded terminal
clusters of orange-red dandelion-type flowers.
Seeds with parachutes are clustered in feathery
hemispheres. Native to alpine Europe, where
it grows up to 2,600m/8,500 ft. Introduced
into UK gardens for its attractive flowers, it
escapes and multiplies prolifically in large
patches by a creeping root system.

GLASSWORT

MARSH SAMPHIRE

Height 15–35cm/6–14in ✿ August–September

Salicornia europaea
L *sal*, salt; *cornis*, horn; *europaea*, European

A fleshy hairless annual. Translucent and
much-branched segmented stems are dark
green at first, turning yellowish with a red
tinge. Insignificant petalless flowers consist
of yellowy stamens in threes up stem and
branches at stem junctions between segments.
   Culpeper says: 'taken in drink purges
melancholy, provokes urine, and expels
dead foetuses. A great quantity taken is
mischievous and deadly; the smell and smoke
of this plant being burnt drives away serpents.'
Ash from burnt stems with sand makes a
coarse glass, hence its common name. An
edible succulent of salt marshes and sandy
shores, but nowadays susceptible to pollution.
Young stems only used for soups, as a
vegetable or a garnish for fish.

GOATSBEARD

JACK-GO-TO-BED-AT-NOON, NAP AT NOON

Height 30–70cm/12–28in ☘ June–July

Tropapogon pratensis
Gk *pogon*, beard; L *pratensis*, of meadows

A perennial and annual herb with a long
brown tap root and a few erect branches
swathed in long, pointed grass-like leaves.
Yellow dandelion-like flowers are borne singly
at the end of stem branches, opening very
early and closing around midday. The fruit is
an attractive 'clock', larger and more open
than dandelion. Seeds are windborne on their
own parachutes.

A detoxicant, it stimulates appetite and
digestion. Its high insulin content makes it
useful for diabetics. Used as a vegetable in
Gerard's time and still used in salads, stews
and soups. The ripe root is treated and eaten
like salsify, stems and young buds like spinach.

GROUNDSEL

ASCENSION, SIMSON, BIRDSEED

Height 7.5–30cm/3–12in ☘ Year-round

Senecio vulgaris
L *senex*, old man (grey haired);
vulgaris, common
AS *grondeswyle*, ground glutton

A very common annual weed of disturbed
ground. Upright irregularly forked weak stems
bear bright green, widely spaced, deeply
toothed leaves. The flowers are borne in
drooping clusters, small, yellow and rayless.
The fruits are in fluffy white heads like
miniature shaving brushes.

Bullein (1562) said: 'the flower of this
herb hath white hayre, and when the wynde
bloweth it away, then it appeareth like a bald-
headed man, therefore it is called senecio.'
Poisonous to humans, it was food for canaries
and rabbits and once a cure for 'staggers' in
horses. Culpeper recommended it especially
as a sore skin poultice.

GROUNDSEL, STICKY
VISCID GROUNDSEL

Height 7.5–20cm/3–8in ❀ July–September

Senecio viscosus
L *senex*, old man; *viscosus*, sticky

Slightly bushy grey-green annual with sticky
hairs all over. Weakly erect, greyish stems bear
deeply and irregularly cut thick leaves. Pale
yellow flowers, fewer than on Groundsel,
are widely conical. Fruits as in Groundsel.
Grows on dry banks, below hedges and on
waste ground. The whole plant is clammy
to the touch.

    Relieves stomach upsets; slightly emetic
but less so than *Senecio vulgaris*. Stops
vomiting. Used to treat ague symptoms.

HAWKBIT, AUTUMNAL
AUTUMN HAWKBIT

Height 10–20cm/4–8in ❀ July–October

Leontodon autumnalis
Gk *leon*, lion; *todon*, tooth; L *autumnalis*,
of autumn

A perennial similar in appearance to a small
Cat's Ear. Rosette of narrow, deeply toothed
leaves with pointed lobes. Branched stems
usually hairless with tiny bracts grouped just
below the flower heads, no white juice or sap.
A single yellow flower is borne on each stem
or branch, dandelion-like, the outer rays
reddish below, with hairy sepal-like pointed
bracts. Seeds on parachutes form a 'clock'.
An upland plant of short, damp grassland.

    Any medicinal use obscure. Hawkbits bear
much honey, which can be smelt in full sun.

HAWKBIT, ROUGH

GREATER HAWKBIT

Height 15–45cm/6–18in ❀ June–October

Leontodon hispidus
Gk *leon*, lion; *todon*, tooth; L *hispidus*, with
coarse bristles

A hairy perennial of lime-rich grassland with
a rosette of rough-toothed leaves. Like all
Hawkbits, it has a leafless, solid stem without
white sap, and is hairy and unbranched.
Yellow dandelion-like flowers with sepal-like
bracts, the outer florets red or orange below,
over 2.5cm/1in across, are held singly. Hairy
seeds form a 'clock'. Its sweet honey-like smell
attracts many insects.

Used like Dandelion and Hawkweeds for
kidney conditions, jaundice and dropsy, and as
a diuretic. The lion's name refers to the leaf
shapes with their 'lion's teeth' edges.

HAWKSBEARD, MARSH

YELLOW SUCCORY, MARSH SUCCORY

Height 22–60cm/9–24in ❀ July–September

Crepis paludosa
Gk *crepis*, boot; L *paludosa*, of marshes

An almost hairless perennial rising from a
rhizome. A solid leafy branched stem without
the milky juice of the Dandelion, it bears
shiny, elliptical, dark green, unstalked, deeply
toothed, spiralling Dandelion-like leaves,
clasping a stem with bases pointing down.
Small Dandelion-like flowers held in loose
terminal sprays with 2 rows of sepal-like
bracts, pointed, with sticky glands. Parachutes
of off-white hairs aid dispersal of narrow seeds.
Can be confused with Hawkweeds, which
have alternate leaves, less deeply toothed.
Common in damp upland places, damp
lowland woods and stream sides or bogs.

HAWKSBEARD, SMOOTH

Height 15–45cm/6–15in ❀ June–November

Crepis capillaris
Gk *crepis*, boot; L *capillaris*, with hairs

A mostly hairless annual of waste places. Smooth, slender stems, branched at bottom or above, bear shiny, lobed, lance-shaped leaves like thin Dandelion leaves. Smaller upper leaves clasp stem below loose clusters of small yellow-petalled Dandelion-like flowers, often reddish below. Seeds have white hairy parachutes for wind dispersal. The commonest lowland grassland Hawksbeard with the smallest flowers.

HENBANE

DEVIL'S EYE, STINKING ROGER

Height 20–80cm/8–32in ❀ June–August

Hyoscyamus niger
Gk *Hyoscyamus*, plant name; L *niger*, black, i.e. poisonous

A hairy, sticky, foul-smelling biennial. Stout hairy round stem bears alternate deeply toothed leaves, stalked at base, upper leaves unstalked. Flowers 2.5cm/1in in diameter grow in long spikes along one side of stem, 5 yellow petals deeply veined in purple, the sepals fused to make a trumpet. Numerous seeds held in a persistent capsule that opens at top when ripe. A rare plant of shingle and sand, common on Walney Island.

A VERY POISONOUS plant which has been used since ancient Assyrian times for toothache and up to the present as a sedative. Contains tannins, atropine, hyoscamine and scropolomine; the source of the drug hyoscine, used by Dr Crippen to poison his wife.

LADY'S MANTLE, SMOOTH

LAMB'S FOOT

Height 5–45cm/2–18in ❀ June–September

Alchemilla glabra
Arab *alkemelych*, alchemist; L *glabra*, smooth,
hairless

A sturdy perennial with a tufted brown stock.
Basal leaves palmate with 7–9 toothed lobes
on hairless stalks. Smooth, slim, branching
stems bear small loose clusters of 4-petalled
yellowish flowers, each set with a ruff-like
bract. Seeds freely. Commonest in Lakes.

According to John Turner (1568): 'In the
night it closeth itselfe together like a purse,
and in the morning it is found full of dew.'
This dew was thought magical. An astringent,
good for skin care and acne. Recommended by
Culpeper it for wounds, bleedings, vomitings,
ruptures, flagging breasts, aiding conception
and retaining foetuses. 'It draws the corruption
from, and heals green wounds; it cures all old
sores, though fistulous and hollow.'

LADY'S MANTLE, YELLOW-GREEN FLOWERED

BEAR'S FOOT

Height 5–45cm/2–18in ❀ May–September

Alchemilla xanthochlora
Arab *alkemelych*, alchemist; L *xantho*, yellow;
chloro, green

A robust tufted perennial, hairy in most parts.
Broad kidney-shaped leaves have a large gap
at the base and are 9-lobed, hairy below,
hairless above. They collect dewdrops at
night. Hairless flower stalks bear dense clusters
of 4-petalled greeny-yellow flowers which seed
prolifically. It grows on damp lowland
roadsides and rich upland pastures and stream
sides.

William Turner called it Our Lady's Mantle,
after the German Frauenmantel or Marien-
mantel. Medicinal uses similar to those of
Alchemilla glabra.

37

LOOSESTRIFE, YELLOW

YELLOW WILLOW-HERB, WILLOW WORT

Height 60–152cm/24–60in ❀ **July–August**

Lysimachia vulgaris
After Lysimachus, a Sicilian king who used it,
or from Gk, to dissolve strife; L *vulgaris*,
common

A softly hairy perennial with opposite or
whorled broad, lance-shaped, short-stalked
leaves, often dotted with dark glands, on erect
hairy stems. Short-stalked, yellow, 5-petalled
flowers are clustered at the tops of stems and
on short branches. Seeds borne in a spherical
capsule. With creeping roots, it forms patches
or clumps.
    As effective for eye complaints as
Eyebright, it was also used to heal open
wounds, to control haemorrhages and
diarrhoea, and as a gargle for quinsy. Bunches
hung between yoked oxen kept them subdued.
It is of the Primrose family, and unrelated to
Purple Loosestrife.

LUPIN, TREE

Height 60–120cm/24–48in ❀ **May–August**

Lupinus arboreus
L *Lupinus*, plant name; *arboreus*, tree-like

A perennial evergreen bush with finger-
shaped leaves divided into 7–11 leaflets,
hairless above, silky below. Yellow pea-flowers
are held in whorls up a fairly stiff spike. Seeds
in pods 4–8cm/1½–3½in long, stiff and hairy.
Grows on sandy soil on Walney Island
and along NW and SW Cumbrian coast.
A rapidly spreading introduction from
California.
    Culpeper says: 'the seeds are somewhat
bitter in taste, opening and cleaning, good to
destroy worms, to bring down the menses, and
expel the birth and secundines. Outwardly
they are used against deformities of the skin,
scabby ulcers, scald heads and other cutaneous
disorders.'

MARIGOLD, MARSH

GOWAN, KINGCUP, MAYBLOB, WATER BLOBS,
MAYFLOWER (SEE NAMING OF PLANTS, PAGE 13)

Height 30–63cm/12–24in ✿ **March–July**

Caltha palustris
L *caltha*, yellow-flowered plant;
palustris, of bogs

A hairless tufted perennial of marsh and damp
woods. Large, glossy, heart- shaped leaves rise
on long stalks from the base. Upper leaves on
hollow flower stems are stalkless. Flowers
2.5cm/1in across or more have glossy yellow
petals with many yellow stamens but no green
sepals. Fruits are a cluster of pods with many
seeds. This plant grew in England before the
Ice Age.

On May Day it was hung over byre doors to
increase the fertility of cattle and keep off evil
spirits. In medieval England it was included in
a cure for eruptive rash. In the USA it is eaten
as a spring vegetable. The petals produce a
yellow dye.

MAYWEED, PINEAPPLE

SCENTED MAYWEED, RAYLESS MAYWEED,
DOG STINKS (CUMBRIA)

Height 5–25cm/2–10in ✿ **June–November**

Chamomilla suaveolons
Gk *chamae*, low-growing; L *suavelons*, frequent

A bushy, hairless, strongly apple-scented
annual with fine 2–3 pinnate segmented
threadlike leaves. The unrayed flower heads
consist of closely bunched 4-toothed yellow-
green florets in an acorn-like cup. Seeds
spread rapidly, so plants are often found in
colonies.

Although seldom used nowadays, once it
was taken for worms, as a sedative and for
relief of spasms. It was taken by settlers to the
USA as Ironwort and made into an ointment
for old sores. Still occasionally used as a tea for
indigestion and insomnia. A pernicious weed,
it blistered hands and feet during harvest.

MONKEY FLOWER

Height 29–45cm/8–18in ✻ July–September

Mimulus guttatus × M. *luteus*
L *mimulus*, little mimic; *guttatus*, spotted;
luteus, deep yellow

A creeping perennial with soft fleshy runners
projecting erect hollow stems at intervals.
Oval serrated shiny leaves borne oppositely,
upper ones unstalked and clasping the stem.
Bright yellow trumpet-shaped flowers rise
individually from leaf joints on slender stalks.
The petal tube is almost closed by 2 small
red-spotted bulges in the throat. Seeds are
produced in a capsule. Thrives in streams,
by streamsides and in other wet places.
Introduced in the early nineteenth century
from the Alaskan Islands off N America. The
flower is supposed to resemble a monkey.

MUGWORT

MUGGERT, MUGWOOD

Height 60–120cm/24–48in ✻ August–September

Artemisia vulgaris
After Gk Artemis, daughter of Zeus and
goddess of wildlife; L *vulgaris*, common
OE Mugwort, midge plant, i.e. deterrent

A perennial plant of waste ground and
quarries, similar to and related to Wormwood.
Stalked lower leaves have toothed deeply cut
pointed leaflets, dark green above with silky
down below. Virtually hairless and with a
musty aroma. Sometimes purplish stems bear
stiffish branches with loose spikes of rayless,
browny-yellow small flowers like tiny buttons,
with cottony bracts.

Artemis said to help women in childbirth;
Roman soldiers used the plant to soothe tired
feet. An antiseptic and vermifuge, slow-acting
tonic and digestive herb; used in proprietary
medicines. Worn by Manx officials at the
Tynwald ceremony against illness and evil.

NIPPLEWORT

Height 22.5–60cm/9–24in ❀ June–October

Lapsana communis
From L *lapsus*, falling; *communis*, common

An annual plant with a many-branched,
upright stem and large, toothed, terminally
pointed oval leaves with smaller lobes or
wings below. Upper leaves are shorter and
lance-shaped. Tough wiry stems are hollow,
but do not have a milky sap. Numerous yellow
flowers are borne erect in loose branched
clusters, from nipple-shaped buds. Brown
curved seeds do not have hairs or parachutes.
Differentiated from Wall Lettuce by the shape
of the leaf.

The Nuremburg physician and botanist
Joachim Camararius in 1588 called this plant
Papillus 'because it is good to heal the ulcers
of the nipples of women's breasts'. John
Parkinson translated this into Nipplewort.
Once used for breast and related ailments.
Also used as a salad plant.

POPPY, WELSH

Height 30–60cm/12–24in ❀ June–August

Mecanopsis cambrica
Gk *mekon*, poppy, *-opsis*, resembling;
L *cambrica*, Welsh

A tufted, slightly hairy perennial with a
carrot-type root. Long-stalked, divided, pale
green leaves bear a yellow sap. Poppy flowers,
yellow or orange, have 4 petals. Seed capsule
hairless, elliptical with a short style at apex.
Seeds released through slits in pod sides, not
from the top as in other poppies. Native to
Wales and SW England, it is now ubiquitous
having spread by garden escapes; most often
seen near houses.

Commonly confused with Californian
Poppy, *Escholtzia*, to which it bears only a
superficial resemblance.

POPPY, YELLOW HORNED
SQUATMOR, BRUISE-ROOT
Height 30–90cm/12–36in   ❀ June–October

Glaucium flavum
Gk *glaukos*, grey-green; L *flavum*, yellow
(paler than *luteum*)

A flamboyant biennial or perennial with
poisonous yellow juice. Stalked, hairy, lobed
lower leaves are wavy and silvery grey. Upper
leaves clasp the stem and are deeply lobed.
Solitary 4-petalled yellow flowers are 5–7.5cm
/2–3in across. A long sickle-shaped seed
capsule (the horn) splits lengthwise to release
seeds. A fairly common plant along the
Cumbrian coast northwards from Humphrey
Head, with northern limit on Solway Firth.

    No longer medicinally popular because
it can affect the brain. Culpeper says: 'it is
sternutatory – the roots ground into snuff
bring on sneezing and the release of water'. He
used it for nervous disorders and as an emetic.

PRIMROSE, EVENING
Height 40–90cm/16–36in   ❀ June–September

Oenothera biennis
Gk *Oenothera*, plant name; L *biennis*, biennial

An erect annual or biennial plant rising from
a large fleshy rootstock. A stout, ridged, hairy
stem bears fine-toothed, crinkly-edged, lance-
shaped leaves, the older ones having red veins.
Erect leafy spikes bear 4-petalled, 4-sepalled
primrose-yellow flowers, up to 5cm/2in across.
Seeds develop on hairy 4-valved cylindrical
flask-shaped cases. Found on Cumbrian coast.

    Introduced in the eighteenth century from
Central America where it was used for coughs
and healing wounds. Oil from the seeds rich
in 2 fatty acids essential to growth and the
reproduction of body cells. Useful for eczema,
pre-menstrual stress, high blood pressure,
alcoholism and multiple sclerosis. Oil also
used in many face creams. The root stock may
be boiled in salt water as a vegetable, but the
leaves must not be eaten.

PURSLANE, SEA

Height 20–45cm/8–18in ❀ July–October

Halimione portulacoides
Gk *Halimione*, daughter of the sea;
L *portulaca*, purslane; Gk *oides*, similar to

A sprawling sturdy sub-shrub. Brown creeping
rooting stems bear alternate silver-grey
untoothed, elliptical leaves, mostly opposite.
The thick fleshy leaves are scaled, bearing sap
to counter the drying effect of salt and wind.
Terminal spikes bear clusters of incurved,
5-petalled yellow flowers. Fruits are in 3-lobed
stalkless bracts. A tough little shrub of salt
marsh, coastal pool and creek, common
around Walney Island and the S Cumbrian
coast.

    The name Purslane is probably a corruption
of porcelain, which it could be said to
resemble.

RAGWORT, MARSH

WATER SEGGRUM

Height 20–30cm/8–12in ❀ May–November

Senecio aquaticus
L *senex*, old man, *aquaticus*, in water

An almost hairless biennial with a reddish
upright, many-branched hairless stem. It bears
deeply divided dark green leaves, the lower
ones unlobed. Bright yellow-rayed flowers
are borne in loose flattish clusters with black-
tipped sepal-like bracts forming a cup to
hold the florets. Usually 12–15 ray florets,
innumerable disc florets. Clearly distinguished
by its reddish stems. Parachute seeds.
Common in wet places on heavy soils or
alluvial silt throughout Europe. Seen in wet
meadows in the Lakes and Dales up to about
400m/1,300ft. Shunned by grazing cattle.

RAGWORT, OXFORD

Height 20–30cm/8–12in　❀ **May–November**

Senecio squalidus
L *senex*, old man; *squalidus*, dirty (flower cups
are blacker than Common Ragwort)

An almost hairless annual or perennial with
an upright, many-branched hairless stem. It
bears deeply divided dark green leaves, the
upper ones clasping the stem. Bright yellow-
rayed flowers are borne in flattish clusters with
black-tipped sepal-like bracts forming a cup
to hold the florets. Usually 13 ray florets,
innumerable disc florets. Parachute seeds.
Distinguished from Common Ragwort, which
has only its inner flower bracts black-tipped,
has narrower petals and more deeply divided
basal leaves. Introduced into botanic gardens
in Oxford and Bideford in 1794, its seeds then
strayed to railway embankments and along
motorways. Commonest in Cumbria along the
M6, as well as in the Dales and along railways.

RATTLE, YELLOW

HEN PEN, PENNY GRASS, HAY RATTLE,
POTS AND PANS

Height 10–60cm/4–24in　❀ **May–August**

Rhinanthus minor
Gk *rhino*, nose; *anthus*, flower (petal tube is
like a hooked nose)

An annual semi-parasite that fixes its roots
on adjacent grasses from which it takes water
and minerals. A single upright stem, often
branched and spotted black, bears opposite
dark green, rough and toothed leaves, rather
like Betony. Yellow hooded flowers are
arranged in opposite pairs above toothed
leaf-like bracts. Open-mouthed flowers bear
2 violet teeth. When ripe, loose seeds rattle
in pods. Quite common in old meadows and
pastures.

　　Gerard records that it was unprofitable,
presumably as a medicine. In Lancashire
bunches of the ripe plants were given to
babies as rattles.

ST JOHN'S WORT, SLENDER

ELEGANT ST JOHN'S WORT

Height 22.5–45cm/9–18in ❀ July–August

Hypericum pulchrum
Gk *hyper*, above; *eikon*, picture; L *pulcher*,
beautiful

A slender ascending perennial of dry acid
soils, often in woodlands. Its rounded smooth
stem often red. Opposite pairs of ovate leaves
have translucent glands. Large narrow heads
of yellow, 5-petalled flowers also have a
reddish tinge. Sepal margins have black
glands. Anthers are orange to reddish-pink;
seeds small and brown.

   Hung up over pictures and doors to drive
away devils and evil spirits. The Knights of
St John of Jerusalem used it to cure wounds
because of its 'signature' perforations in the
leaves, resembling wounds. Common St John's
Wort (*Hypericum perforatum*) more commonly
used as herbal medicine.

SOW-THISTLE, SMOOTH

SOW-THISTLE, SWINE THISTLE, MILK THISTLE,
HARE'S HOUSE

Height 20–152cm/8–60in ❀ June–August

Sonchus oleraceous
L *Sonchus*, plant family name; *oleraceous*,
kitchen pot herb

A hairless greyish annual of disturbed ground.
Upright, with few branches, smooth stems and
rich in milky sap. Pinnately lobed, flat, broad-
toothed leaves clasp stems with pointed,
arrow-shaped basal lobes and a winged stalk.
Yellow flowers like Dandelions borne in
terminal clusters. Clocks of seeds with long
white hairs as parachutes.

   The milky juice was used to increase
mothers' milk, for stomach problems,
wheezing, haemorrhoids, deafness and as
a skin lotion. In 1690 John Ray said some
people used it as a salad or a vegetable 'but we
leave it for hares and rabbits'. It is still used in
salads or like spinach.

TANSY

BACHELORS' BUTTONS

Height 25–90cm/10–36in ❁ July–September

Tanacetum vulgare
L *tanacetum*, immortality; *vulgare*, common

A sturdy dark perennial with an erect stem, tinged red and branched above. Sharply toothed leaves resemble fishbones or ferns – 2 rows of up to 12 deeply toothed leaflets arranged spirally up the stem. Rayless yellow button-like flowers in large flat-topped clusters. Seeds dry with few hairs.

Culpeper says: 'A carminative and destroyer of worms. The leaves are used to stop all kinds of fluxes, to congeal blood, etc.' He recommends it for bruises, freckles, sunburn, gripe, sciatica and joint aches. Its bitter 'absinthin' can cause brain damage. Used in France in omelettes and cakes, but forbidden in aperitifs and other alcoholic drinks.

TOADFLAX

FLAX WEED, GALLWORT, BUTTER AND EGGS, BUNNY MOUTHS

Height 23–76cm/9–30in ❁ July–October

Linaria vulgaris
L *linaria*, flax; *vulgaris*, common
AS toad, worthless (cf dog or horse)

A blue-green perennial with erect stems rising from a creeping rootstock. Alternate lance-shaped leaves bear basal bracts. Yellow snapdragon flowers hug a tight spike. Each flower has a 3-lobed tube, with two orange spots, that ends in a long spur, and a 2-lobed upper petal. Oval capsules containing flattened winged seeds are larger than the corolla.

A diuretic and purgative that induces perspiration. Essence used for diarrhoea and cystitis; also for jaundice, constipation, dropsy and haemorrhoids. Culpeper says it was put into chickens' water 'to cure them of gall and to relieve them when drooping'.

TOUCH-ME-NOT

OLD WOMAN'S PURSE

Height 20–152cm/8–60in ❀ July–September

Impatiens noli-tangere
L *impatiens*, explosive; *noli-tangere*,
do not touch

Hairless, erect, almost translucent reddish
stems bear alternate elliptical, toothed leaves.
Yellow drooping flowers with reddish spots
hang in loose bunches, the lower sepals like a
sac with a down-curved spur. Seeds in an
explosive capsule. Latin name derives from
Christ's words to Mary Magdalene after his
resurrection: 'Noli me tangere' (John XX:17).
Balsams are impatient! If touched when ripe,
seeds are ejected forcibly from capsules. An
annual of damp places, woods and streamsides
in partial shade, the only native British
Balsam, found in Cumbria and N Wales alone.
   A strong emetic. Weak decoctions
occasionally used for haemorrhoids and
as a laxative and diuretic.

TREFOIL, HOP

HOP CLOVER, CRAID (SCOTLAND)

Height 20–53cm/8–23in ❀ May–September

Trifolium campestre
L *tri*, three; *folium*, leaf (shamrock-type leaves
have 3 leaflets); *campestre*, of lowland plains

A short hairy erect annual. Trefoil (3-lobed)
leaves, leaflets oval, narrowing towards the
base, the central one larger. Yellow balls of
flowers like Black Medick turn white from the
outsides to brown as hop-like seeds develop
into a drooping bunch. Called Hop Trefoil or
Hop Clover because dying flower heads
change from yellow to white to brown, and
look like miniature hop cones. Can be
confused with Black Medick, which is downy
with stalked yellow flowers that drop when
dead to reveal black pods. An animal fodder
plant.

VETCH, KIDNEY

LADIES' FINGERS, LADY'S SLIPPER,
CRAE NEBS (CROW NOSE, NORTHUMBERLAND)

Height 10–60cm/4–24in ❀ **May–September**

Anthyllis vulneraria
Gk *Anthyllis*, plant name; L *vulneratus*,
wounded, damaged

An upright perennial with silky stems and
leaves. Leaves made up of a large terminal
leaflet and 4–5 opposite lance-shaped leaflets.
Yellow flower heads are borne erect on a long
stem, densely packed together, with leaf-like
bracts forming a containing ruff. The flowers
turn brown to expose fluffy pods containing
seeds. Prefers a rich, limy soil.

Astringent and mildly purgative. Used for
wounds, cuts, burns and skin eruptions (Latin
name), and to cure kidney ailments (English
name). The dried flower heads can make a tea
substitute. A mild infusion may be taken as a
spring tonic or against constipation.

VETCHLING, MEADOW

MEADOW PEA, LADY'S SLIPPER

Height 30–120cm/12–48in ❀ **June–August**

Lathyrus pratensis
Gk *lathyrus*, pea; L *pratensis*, meadow

A sprawling shrubby perennial of grassy
places, hedges, woods and verges. A creeping
root-stock throws up many clump-forming
shoots. Its weak square stems bear tendrils, but
support themselves mainly on nearby grasses.
Lance-shaped leaves are in pairs, each with a
weak tendril, and leaf-like arrow-shaped bracts
at the base. 6–12 pea flowers are borne on
long stalks rising above other vegetation.
Hairless seeds in flattish pods. This member of
the pea family is often sown as a fodder crop
and to enrich the soil, root nodules producing
nitrogen to aid the growth of other plants such
as cereal crops.

WATER LILY, YELLOW

BRANDY BOTTLE, WATERBLOBS

Height 5–20cm/2–8in ❀ June–September

Nuphar lutea
Arab *Nuphar*, plant name; L *lutea*, yellow

A perennial rising from rhizomes rooted in
lake beds. Large oval leathery leaves float on
the water surface with a few cabbage-like
leaves below. Yellow brandy-bowl flowers rise
on branched stems just above the surface, and
have a faint alcoholic smell. Air bladders in
the plant keep it afloat until decay. Seeds
borne in carafe-shaped capsules. The largest
yellow aquatic flower of still or slow fresh
water. Common in SW Cumbria and the
Dales.

Medicinal uses remote – allegedly it was
used to reduce the sex urge and encourage
celibacy. The rhizomes, dipped in tar, were
applied to arrest or even cure baldness.

WELD

DYER'S WEED, YELLOW WEED, DYER'S ROCKET,
YELLOW ROCKET

Height 50–152cm/20–60in ❀ June–September

Reseda luteola
L *resedo*, to heal; *luteola*, yellow

A tall hairless biennial with alternate, lance-
shaped, unlobed leaves with wavy edges.
Flowers are a spike of yellowish-green 4-
petalled and 4-sepalled flowers. Upright
seed pods divided into pointed lobes. Flowers
heliotropic, i.e. they follow the sun round
the horizon by day, even in cloud.

From Morocco northwards it was used as
a fast yellow dye, being known even in Stone
Age Switzerland. It took 3–6 plants to dye
450g/1lb of cloth, fixed with alum, and was
widely used in medieval England where it was
commonly cultivated near mills. Quoted by
Chaucer as a dyer's plant, along with Madder
and Woad.

WINTERCRESS

YELLOW ROCKET

Height 30–90cm/12–36in ❀ **May–September**

Barbarea vulgaris
After St Barbara, patron saint of quarrymen,
miners and gunners; L *vulgaris*, common

A hairless biennial or perennial of riversides,
roadsides and disturbed ground. A small
yellowish tap root feeds a rosette of deeply
lobed lyre-shaped leaves. Upper leaves clasp
the stem alternately. Yellow 4-petalled flowers
are borne in dense branched spikes that
lengthen as the fruits develop. Petals are twice
as long as sepals. Long narrow seed pods have
short beaks.
A plant rich in Vitamin C. Basal leaves
used in winter as spinach, in spring for
salads. Plants are still bright and green on
4 December, St Barbara's day. Now replaced
as a salad plant by the less bitter Watercress.

BINDWEED, GREAT

LARGE BINDWEED

Length 90–240cm/36–96in ❀ July–September

Calystegia sylvatica
Gk *kalyx*, cup; *stege*, covered; L *sylvatica*,
of woods

A spreading perennial with creeping roots.
Long twining stems bear green arrow-shaped
leaves and large white funnel-shaped flowers
6–7.5cm/2½–3in across, sometimes pink-
striped, with 2 large red-veined bracts
enveloping the calyx. Flowers stay open till
nightfall, or all night in a full moon. If closed,
they burst open at daybreak. Fruits form a
globular capsule. Always twines anti-
clockwise.

  Extract from milky roots of Bindweeds from
Syria used as a purgative in Pliny's time, but
frequent fatalities caused its discontinuance.
Gerard declares it is very dangerous, especially
if taken from some 'runnagat physic-monger',
'quack salver' or other 'abusers of physick.'

BINDWEED, HEDGE

SCAMMONY, MORNING GLORY, GREATER BINDWEED, BELLVINE, ROPE-BIND

Length up to 300cm/120in ❀ July–September

Calystegia sepium
Gk *kalyx*, cup; *stege*, covered; L *sepium*,
of hedges

A low, spreading perennial with long creeping
roots. Long twining stems bear alternate green
arrow- or heart-shaped leaves and white
funnel-shaped flowers up to 5cm/2in across,
the seed case shielded by 2 narrower bracts.
Fruits in a globular capsule. Always twines
anti-clockwise. Stems up to 320cm/120in
long, but can scramble much higher up trees.
The twisting woody stems persist a long time
and gave rise to one of its vernacular names,
Rope-Bind.

  As with Great Bindweed, a very strong
purgative, not to be used by those of a delicate
constitution.

BITTERCRESS, HAIRY

Height 7.5–15cm/3–6in   ✤ **February–November**

Cardamine hirsuta
Gk *cardamine*, a similar plant; L *hirsuta*, hairy

A small hairy annual. A rosette of slender pinnate leaves (a terminal ivy-shaped leaflet and 4 opposite pairs of smaller heart-shaped leaflets), slightly hairy both sides, cradles a very hairy erect stem with a few slender leaves. Several 4-petalled white flowers top each stem or branch. Tall slender seed pods overtop flower heads and explode when ripe. The similar Shepherd's Cress is usually hairless, with seed pods like small Shepherd's Purse pods. A common weed of gardens and dry places.

Culinary use doubtful, but it can give a tang to spring salads.

BITTERCRESS, VARIANT

Height 25–45cm/10–18in   ✤ **May–June**

Cardamine pratensis
Gk *cardamine*, name of a similar plant;
L *pratensis*, of meadows

A hairless perennial rising from a slender creeping rootstock. Angular stem bears leaves like watercress; fleshy, oval, pale green leaflets, almost opposite, rising to a single oval terminal. Upper leaves with narrower, sometimes toothed, leaflets. White or purplish 4-petalled flowers with purple anthers held in a loose head. Seeds along a narrow beaked pod. Scattered through the damp lowlands of the Lake District, especially Windermere, and lime-rich valleys of the Yorkshire Dales, possibly an introduced Continental variant.

Similar uses to Milkmaids (*Cardamine pratensis*) – diuretic, relieves spasms and helps scurvy – but not so effective. Can be used as a salad ingredient, but tastes too bitter for most people.

BITTERCRESS, WAVY

Height 10–29cm/4–8in ✿ April–August

Cardamine flexuosa
Gk *cardamine*, a similar plant; L *flexuosa*, zigzag

A biennial or perennial, slightly taller than
Hairy Bittercress, with a basal rosette of hairy
leaves, sprawling, similar to but larger than
Hairy Bittercress with more stem leaves. Erect
hairy zigzag stem, much branched, carries 4-
petalled white flowers with 6 stamens (4 in
Hairy Bittercress). Tall slim fruit pods do not
overtop flowerbuds. Common throughout the
area in damp places, often in shade.

  Culinary use limited but can be added to
spring salads.

BRAMBLE

BLACKBERRY, BRUMMEL ('PRICKLY')

Stems up to 180cm/72in long ✿ May–September

Rubus fruticosus
L *rubus*, plant name; *fruticosus*, shrubby

A deciduous scrambling woody shrub armed
with sharp thorns on biennial stems that often
root at the tips. Prickly 3 or 5-lobed leaflets
are toothed, roundish, and hairy below. White
or pink 5-petalled flowers develop into green
fleshy clusters that turn a shiny black as they
ripen. Flowers on second-year stems.

  The leaves and root bark can be used to
assuage diarrhoea, dysentery and whooping
cough. Bramble jelly was once used to treat
dropsy. Fleshy fruits used for jams and wine.
Leaves. dried and fermented, make a good tea,
and have also been used as a black hair dye.

BRAMBLE, STONE

ROEBUCK BERRY

Height 15-25cm/6–10in   ✿ June–August

Rubus saxatilis
L *rubus*, plant name, Bramble family;
saxatilis, of stony places

A low creeping sub-shrub of the Bramble family with a thin, prickly, scrambling stem bearing toothed 3-part leaves. Upright stems bear loose clusters of small off-white flowers with narrow petals and recurved sepals. Red fruits (inset) have few large succulent segments. Grows in shaded rock crevices and other lime-rich areas up to 750m/2450ft. Also found in Freeholders Wood, Carperby (see Walk 14, Volume 1, *Limestone Flowers*). Fruit similar in appearance to Dewberry, but with bright red, not bloomed black segments.

Medicinal and culinary uses as for Bramble.

BUTTERBUR, WHITE

Height 15–39cm/6–12in   ✿ January–March

Petasites albus
Gk *petasos*, hot; L *albus*, white

A perennial with a stout creeping rootstock from which flower spikes rise regularly. Long-stalked white flowers precede leaves in a broad spike similar to a hyacinth. It is delicately perfumed. Green bracts up the stalk are rolled inwards. The flowers are followed by round, heart-shaped, toothed leaves, woolly beneath. An escaped introduction from N Europe, most prominent in S Lakeland near to habitations.

The leaves and roots have a slightly peppery flavour. In Cumbria the leaves were used to wrap butter.

CAMPION, BLADDER

SPATLING POPPIE

Height 25–90cm/10–36in ❀ May–September

Silene vulgaris
Gk *Silene*, plant name; L *vulgaris*, common

An upright hairless perennial with a greyish
look to its foliage. All stems bear opposite
pointed oval leaves with hairy margins and
a terminal spray of distinctive white flowers
with deeply lobed petals. The net-veined
sepals that form the inflated calyx are pinched
in below the 5 petals to form the bladder.
Seeds are globular. A common plant of drier
ground where there is little competition from
tall grasses. The flowers emit a clove-like
perfume in the evening; bumble bees unable
to enter the narrow-necked calyx bite holes
in the sides to get at the nectar.

The leaves and young shoots before
flowering can be used in salads or added
to soups and sauces.

CAMPION, SEA

Height up to about 15cm/6in ❀ June–August

Silene maritima
Gk *silene*, campion; L *maritima*, seaside

A sprawling hairless greyish perennial that
forms low mats or tufts. Hairless unbranched
shoots, some flowering, others non-flowering,
bear opposite pairs of unstalked thickish fleshy
leaves. Single or few large white flowers have
overlapping, deeply notched petals in an
inflated, veined cup with 6 points. Seeds in a
pumpkin-shaped capsule. Grows in shingle or
sand, usually on the drift line, but also on
inland screes and cliffs.

Once used to stem bleeding, give relief
to kidney stones, help old sores and combat
snake bites and plague. Also used as a
vegetable with a pea-like flavour.

CHICKWEED

CHICKENWEED (CUMBRIA, YORKSHIRE,
SCOTLAND)

Height 5–40cm/2–16in ❀ March–November

Stellaria media
L *stellaria*, starry; *media*, middle-sized

A sprawling pale wintergreen annual.
Frequently-branched round stems have line of
hairs down one side, alternately between leaf
nodes. Pointed oval leaves in opposite pairs,
lower ones stalked; stalkless upper leaves close
at night to protect the tender shoots. Tiny
white 5-petalled flowers, petals deeply cleft,
with equal-length sepals forming a star.
Reddish seeds in drooping capsules.

   Dioscorides prescribed it for eye and ear
problems. It soothes irritated skin, eczema,
varicose veins and nettle rash, and as an
ointment eases ulcers, chilblains and sore
throats. Useful salad or vegetable plant, but
excess causes diarrhoea and vomiting.

CLOVER, WHITE

LAMB SUCKLINGS (CUMBERLAND AND
YORKSHIRE), MUTTON ROSE, DUTCH CLOVER

Height 10–50cm/4–20in ❀ June–September

Trifolium repens
L *tri*, three; *folium*, leaved; *repens*, creeping

A perennial with creeping stems that root
at nodes forming mats. Stalked leaves are a
typical shamrock shape, but smaller than Red
Clover. Scented white flowers arranged in
dense globular heads. Fruit is a flattened linear
pod with up to 6 seeds. Rich in pollen.

   Used like Red Clover as a tea substitute,
the leaves for salads or as a vegetable like
spinach. The tenth-century Welsh text *The
Mabinogian* describes Olwen as 'a girl with
breasts whiter than a white swan's breasts,
cheeks redder than the Foxglove, and hair
more yellow than the flowers of the Broom.
White Clover plants would spring up in her
footprints wherever she walked.' Olwen means
white footprint.

DEADNETTLE, WHITE

WHITE ARCHANGEL (YORKSHIRE),
ADAM AND EVE IN THE BOWER (SOMERSET)

Height 20–60cm/8–24in ❀ May–December

Lamium album
L *lamium*, nettle; *album*, white

A hairy faintly aromatic creeping perennial,
usually in wide colonies. Square, hollow, hairy
stems bear opposite pairs of toothed, heart-
shaped leaves like Stinging Nettle on short
stalks. Whorls of white flowers rise from leaf
nodes, upper lip hairy, lower has a large
notched middle lobe and 2 smaller lateral
lobes. (Turn the flower upside down and under
the white upper lip of the corolla the black
and gold stamens, side by side, are Adam and
Eve.) Fruits are 4 nutlets in the sepal tube.

Once used against diarrhoea, varicose
veins, haemorrhoids, scrofula and to reduce
menstrual bleeding.

DEWBERRY

Height 20–60cm/8–24in ❀ May–September

Rubus caesius
L *rubus*, plant name, Bramble family;
caesius, lavender blue

A weak sprawling sub-shrub, similar to
Bramble. Round stems, grey when young,
bear short weak bristles. Trifoliate leaves are
wrinkled, sharply toothed with oval leaflets.
White flowers, larger than Bramble, in small
loose clusters with long slim sepals, which do
not turn down as with Brambles. Edible fruits
like Brambles, but fewer, with larger segments,
bloomed like sloes. A plant of damp limestone
grassland or dune slacks, common in Cumbria,
including Walney Island, but more localised in
the Dales.

The Romans used this as lavender-blue eye
make-up.

ELDER

COMMON ELDER

Height 2–10m/6¹/₂–32ft ❀ June–July

Sambucus nigra
L *sambucus* from Gk *sambuca*, sackbut;
L *nigra*, black, i.e. poisonous

A deciduous shrub or small tree with a cork-like greyish bark and opposite leaves divided into 3–5 toothed leaflets. Large flat-topped umbrellas of heavily scented white flowers turn into bunches of fleshy drupes.

    Despite all the green parts being poisonous the Elder has innumerable uses. The flowers and berries make a drug that induces perspiration, and the leaves prepared as an ointment are used for bruises, sprains, swellings and chilblains (older readers may recall Zambuk ointment). The flowers and berries are also used for wines and desserts. Elder features strongly in folklore, representing sorrow and death. The Russians believed it drove away evil spirits.

ELDER, GROUND

BISHOP'S WEED, GOUTWEED, GOATWEED

Height 30–60cm/12–24in ❀ May–July

Aegopodium podograria
Gk *aigos*, goat; *podos*, foot (from leaf);
podogra, gout

A hairless, creeping, invasive perennial. Hollow, smooth, grooved stems bear leaves similar to Elder, one terminal leaflet and up to 4 pairs of opposite leaflets. Dense umbrellas of small white flowers are borne on up to 20 short stems at the top of an erect flower stem. Egg-shaped seeds are ridged. Commonest near habitations where it was once cultivated.

    An introduced plant once used like spinach and as a medicinal source. Culpeper recommended it for gout, as suggested by its species name, and sciatica; also for joint aches and other cold pains. By Gerard's time it was acknowledged as a serious garden pest.

FEVERFEW

Height 25–60cm/10–24in ✿ **July–August**

Tanacetum parthenium
L *Tanacetum*, medieval plant name;
Gk *parthenos*, maidens

A downy perennial with erect stems bearing
spirally, pinnately divided yellowish-green,
toothed, aromatic leaves. Upper part of stem
branched. Branches bear loose flat-topped
clusters of daisy-like flowers, yellow with
white rays. Ribbed brown seeds have papery
edges.

Once in common use, and still used now
as an insect repellant and for headaches and
migraine. Gerard said: 'It purgeth melancholie
and phlegm . . . good for them that are giddie
in the head or have vertigo. Also good for
such as be sad, pensive, and without speech.'
Culpeper says: 'Venus has commended it to
her sisters [women] to be a general strengthener
of wombs and to remedy such infirmities as a
careless midwife has there caused.'

FOOL'S WATERCRESS

BROOKLIME

Height 30–90cm/12–36in ✿ **July–August**

Apium nodiflorum
L *apium*, celery or parsnip; *nodiflorum*, flowers
coming from nodes

A sprawling hairless perennial with a furrowed
weak stem that grows in wet rich soils. Leaves
are 1-pinnate with 5–13 toothed, pointed-
oval, opposite leaflets. Small white 5-petalled
flowers with prominent pink stamens form an
umbrella-shaped head. Fruits are oval ridged
seeds. Commonly found in wet lowland areas
in Cumbria, and while rarer in the Yorkshire
Dales it is found growing beside Watercress in
Wharfedale.

Culpeper recommended it in a diet drink
of mixed cresses. It has many similarities with
Watercress, and although a poor substitute it
is edible especially if cooked with meat.

GIPSYWORT

GIPSYWEED, WATER HOREHOUND,
EGYPTIAN'S HERB

Height 30–100cm/12–40in ❀ June–September

Lycopus europaeus
L *lycopus*, wolf's foot; *europaeus*, European

An upright, slightly hairy perennial, like a
Mint but scentless. Pairs of broad, deeply
toothed dandelion-like leaves rotate right up
the stiffish branched stems with dense whorls
of small white flowers, bell-shaped and purple-
dotted at the upper leaf bases. Calyx has spiny
teeth that hold seed nutlets.

Its common names derive from its use by
gipsies and vagabonds as a dye to darken the
skin, to elicit greater sympathy and thereby
attract more alms. The black dye it produced
was used as a fast dye for silks and wool. It was
used rarely as an astringent and as a sedative.
It has no culinary value.

HELLEBORINE, MARSH

Height 10–45cm/4–18in ❀ July – August

Epipactis palustris
L Epipactis, name of all but three of the
British Helleborines; *palustris*, marsh

A perennial orchid with a creeping
underground rootstock (like Lily of the
Valley), thin and much-branched. About 6
pointed oval leaves are arranged round the
base of the stem, with 2–4 smaller ones up
stem. A short flower spike bears about 10
flowers with a white notched almost frilly lip,
crimson and white within, and with purplish-
brown sepals. The notched lip is usually
horizontal, and it falls when an insect lands on
it, springing back when it takes off. A downy
pear-shaped seed capsule hangs down. A plant
of rich damp grassland and especially coastal
dune slacks. There are large localised
communities on North Walney Island.

HOGWEED

KECK, KESH (N ENGLAND), COW PARSNIP

Height 60–120cm/24–48in ❀ June–September

Heracleum sphondylium
After Heracles (Hercules), who used it
medicinally; L *sphondylium*, rounded

A stout hairy perennial with tall hollow
ridged stems. Large hairy pinnate leaves have
coarsely toothed leaflets – terminal and
opposite pairs – with stalks sheathing stems.
Large flattened umbrellas of up to 20 branched
bunches of white flowers with irregular outer
florets. Seeds are oval to round, flattened, with
a slight wing on sides.

Culpeper says the seeds are useful for
coughs, shortness of breath, falling sickness,
jaundice, phlegm and liver problems. Seeds
and roots boiled in oil and rubbed on the head
help frenzy, lethargy and shingles; flower juice
cleans runny ears. Extracts still used in
proprietary medicines for laryngitis and
bronchitis. Once fed to pigs.

HOGWEED, GIANT

CARTWHEEL FLOWER

Height to 30cm/120in ❀ June–July

Heracleum mantegazzianum
After Heracles (Hercules) and Paolo
Mantegazzi (1831–1910)

A tall stately biennial with red-spotted, sturdy,
ridged stems up to 300cm/10ft high. Long-
stalked leaves, pinnate with broad-toothed
and lobed leaflets, blade and leaf of equal
length, can be up to 90cm/3ft long. Umbrellas
of white flowers similar to Hogweed can
measure up to 50cm/20in across. Prolific seeds
dispersed by currents along rivers and streams.
Once common beside the lower R Kent and
the middle R Eden. Eradication constantly
pursued.

A most attractive noxious weed of
riversides and streamsides. Its stems create
a traumatic photo-allergenic effect on the
skin, so should be shunned, especially in
pea-shooters!

KALE, SEA

Height 20–60cm/8–24in ❀ March–May

Crambe maritima
Gk *crambe*, cabbage; L *maritima*, growing
by the sea

A clumped perennial with a fleshy, branched
root. Stout, erect, hairless stems bear large,
fleshy, blue-green leaves with crinkly lobes up
to 30cm/12in long. White 4-petalled flowers
are borne erect in a broad cluster, like a
cauliflower gone to seed. Globular seed pods;
seeds dispersed by sea. Fairly common along
the S Cumbrian coast westward round to
Bardsea. A coastal plant of dunes and shingle
beaches, therefore none in the land-locked
Yorkshire Dales.

Young shoots and leaves can be blanched,
boiled and eaten plain, or minced and
flavoured with garlic.

KNOTGRASS

PIG GRASS (YORKSHIRE), IRON GRASS,
SWINE'S GRASS (NORTHUMBERLAND)

Height 5–30cm/2–12in ❀ June–October

Polygonum aviculare
Gk *poly*, many; *gony*, knee; L *aviculare*,
bird (food for)

A sprawling perennial with creeping stems up
to 180cm/72in. Upright flowering stems bear
alternate lance-shaped leaves with small
brown sheaths where they join the main stem.
Clusters of about 6 pinky-white 5-petalled
flowers develop into 3-sided nutlets. The
species name refers to its attraction for small
birds that feed on it.

Used as a diuretic in China for over 2,000
years. Dioscorides prescribed it for its diuretic
properties, for menstrual bleeding and for
snake bite. It has been used for ulcers and
sores, and for pigs off their food. Included
in some herbal teas.

MAYWEED, SEA

SCENTLESS MAYWEED

Height 15–45cm/6–18in ❀ July–September

Matricaria maritima
L *matricalis*, mother (caring for);
maritima, of the sea

A hairless sprawling annual or perennial
with deeply divided slender leaves that end
in a point. Flat, daisy-like flower-heads have
white rays surrounding crowded yellow florets.
Ripening fruits form a solid cone of brown
seeds. Related to Chamomile, which it
resembles. Often found in large clumps
among shingle.

Called Mayweed because it was helpful to
maidens (nothing to do with the month of
May); it was used for all kinds of female
complaints.

MOUSE-EAR

MOUSE-EAR CHICKWEED

Height 10–25cm/4–10in ❀ April–November

Cerastium fontanum
Gk *keros*, horn (capsule shape), L *fontanus*,
near water

A hairy perennial of the chickweed family,
slightly tufted, with short non-flowering
shoots and upright flowering shoots.
Unstalked lance-shaped hairy leaves in
opposite pairs up stem, upper ones may have
white edges. Loose clusters of 5-petalled
notched white flowers with 5 green sepals of
same length as petals forming a white and
green star. Curved seed capsule. A common
plant up to 900m/3,000ft.

Culpeper says it 'helps jaundice; good
against stones and gripe; stays blood flows;
syrup of the juice and sugar for coughs, cuts
and wounds. The juice stays fretting cancers
and ulcers in the mouth and secret parts.'

MOUSE-EAR, STICKY

Height 12.5–30cm/5–12in ❀ April–November

Cerastium glomeratum
Gk *keros*, horn (seed capsule); L *glomeratum*,
closely grouped

A hairy, sticky annual, more prominent than
common Mouse-ear. Hairy, yellowish-green
stems bear pairs of hairy, yellowish-green
opposite oval leaves, the upper ones not
white-edged. White flowers on erect stems in
compact leafy clusters, smaller than Mouse-
ear, the petals shallowly notched. Common in
lowland pastures, tracksides and verges. More
conspicuous than Mouse-ear.
    Medicinal properties similar to Mouse-ear.

NIGHTSHADE, BLACK

GARDEN NIGHTSHADE (S ENGLAND)

Height up to 60cm/24in ❀ July–October

Solanum nigrum
L *solanum*, solace (medicinal); *nigrum*, black

An erect, non-woody, usually hairless annual.
Blackish stems bear pointed oval, slightly
lobed, stalked leaves. Clusters of 5–10 flowers
with pointed white petals and prominent
yellow anthers are carried up the stem. Fruit is
a green round berry which turns black when
ripe. A southern wasteland plant, but grows in
the Eden Valley, along the coast, and in some
profusion on South Walney Island.
    Its solanine and saponin make it useful for
treating spasms and epilepsy and as a sedative.
The berries are believed to be poisonous, and
cattle and sheep avoid it. More powerful and
more narcotic than Woody Nightshade
(*Solanum dulcamara*).

PARSLEY, COW

KECK (CUMBERLAND), QUEEN ANNE'S LACE,
BAD MAN'S OATMEAL (NORTHUMBERLAND,
YORKSHIRE)

Height 60–120cm/24–48in ❀ April–June

Anthriscus sylvestris
L *Anthriscus*, plant name; *sylvestris*, woodland

A sturdy perennial with upright furrowed
stems, downy below, hairy above. Fresh, finely
cut leaves have toothed segments not unlike
Sweet Cicely but not aromatic, and unspotted.
Upper stem branched, with smooth-stalked
globular flower-heads forming a flattish
umbrella. Fruits are smooth and long, broad at
the base, with a short beak at the tip. The
commonest white umbellifer of road verges
and hedge bottoms in late spring. Can be
mistaken for Hemlock and Fool's Parsley,
both poisonous.

    Few uses: leaves fed to rabbits, stems
used for pea-shooters. Has superstitious
connections with the Devil.

ROCKCRESS, HAIRY

Height 15–45cm/6–18in ❀ May–August

Arabis hirsuta
L *Arabis*, plant probably from Arabia;
hirsuta, hairy

A hairy biennial with a sturdy rosette of hairy,
slightly toothed spoon-shaped leaves. Tall
hairy stem clad spirally by clasping hairy
toothed leaves. Through a magnifying glass
the dense hairs are seen to be forked. White
4-petalled flowers borne on a long terminal
spike. Fruits in pods, upright and close to the
stem. A common plant in limestone areas,
often found growing on walls, rocks and
bridges, but also found in some Silurian areas.

    No known medicinal use.

ROSE, BURNET

CAT WHIN (YORKSHIRE, NORTHUMBERLAND)

Height up to 100cm/40in ❀ May–July

Rosa pimpinellifolia
L *rosa*, rose; *pimpinellifolia*, leaves like
pimpinella (twice pinnate as in Salad Burnet,
formerly called *Pimpinella sanguisorbia*)

A suckering deciduous shrub of dry rich
ground. Upright, branching, very spiny stems
bear leaves like Burnet Saxifrage or Salad
Burnet, a small, toothed, oval terminal leaflet
and 6–8 opposite pairs of similar leaflets.
Solitary creamy-white flowers are quite
fragrant. Fruits are small seeds in round
purple-black 'hips'.

Once called *Rosa spinosissima*, the spiniest
of all roses. Perhaps so, but also the sweetest
smelling, with a scent like a mixture of honey
and jasmine. The juice of the fruit makes a
peach dye or, mixed with alum, a violet dye.

ROSE, FIELD

Height 100–200cm/40–80in ❀ June–August

Rosa arvensis
L *arvensis*, of fields

A scrambling deciduous shrub with weak
green stems and few hooked thorns. Hairless,
toothed, elliptical leaflets on typical stalked
rose leaves. Large white bowl-shaped flowers
borne singly or in twos or threes have a stout
column and crowded yellow stamens. Flowers
later and longer than Dog Rose. Fruits are red
roundish hips, smaller than those of the Dog
Rose. Despite its name, most often seen
scrambling through small trees in woods or in
hedgerows, usually on heavy soils. Not as
sweetly scented as its commoner cousin, it is
less often used. It soon loses its petals, and is
therefore unsatisfactory as a cut flower.

SANDWORT, SEA

Height 5–25cm/2–10in   ☀ May–September

Honkenya peploides
After G. A. Honkenya, German botanist
(1724–1805); L *pepo*, pumpkin;
Gk *-oides*, resembling (the seed pods look
like tiny pumpkins or spurge-like)

A hairless, sprawling, fleshy perennial rooting
at nodes. Yellowish, pointed oval, succulent
opposite leaves in rows up stem. Separate sex
greeny-white flowers borne in leaf clusters or
on short stalks. Large yellow-green fruits like
small pumpkins hold seeds. A sturdy low
colonising plant of shifting sandy beaches and
dunes. Its fleshy leaves make it tolerant of salt,
sand and winds. Frequently rooting, it forms
broad mats that can endure inundation by
water and covering with sand to build up little
dunes of their own.
   Medicinal or culinary uses, if any, are
obscure.

SAXIFRAGE, MEADOW

CUCKOO FLOWER (YORKSHIRE), PRETTY MAIDS,
DRY CUCKOOS (WET CUCKOOS, MILKMAIDS)

Height 10–50cm/4–20in   ☀ April–June

Saxifraga granulata
L *saxum*, rock; *frago*, break; *granulata*, with
little knobs

A downy perennial of dry meadows. Stalked,
gently lobed kidney-shaped lower leaves clasp
the stem. A single straight hairy stem, tending
to wave after branching, bears a few similar
leaves and loose clusters of 5-petalled, green-
veined white flowers in a hairy 5-sepal cup. A
long-horned fruit splits to release seeds. Also
reproduces by small bulbils at the base of the
plant, hence the species name *granulata*.
   According to Culpeper, 'an excellent
diuretic; an infusion of the whole plant
operates powerfully and safely by urine, and
clears the passages from gravel'. In the garden
these are the 'Pretty Maids' of 'Mary, Mary,
quite contrary'.

SHEPHERD'S PURSE

BAD MAN'S OATMEAL (NE ENGLAND),
MOTHER'S HEART (LANCASHIRE)

Height 7.5–45cm/3–18in ✸ March–October

Capsella bursa-pastoris
L *capsella*, capsule; *bursa*, purse; *pastoris*,
shepherd or poor countryman

A low downy annual with a rosette of
both slightly and deeply lobed leaves like
Dandelion. Toothed upper leaves, arrow-
shaped at base, clasp stem. Flowers in erect
spike, opening progressively upward. Fruits
are in an elongated heart shape (the purse).

As tea, a diuretic and a cure for nosebleeds
and heavy uterine bleeds; it is recommended
to mix it with Pellitory of the Wall and
Juniper to disguise its bitter taste. In the First
World War it was used on the front to staunch
bleeding. In China, used for dysentery,
diarrhoea and eye troubles. Essences used
in some proprietary medicines. Young leaves
are used in salads, sauces and soups.

STITCHWORT, GREATER

HEADACHE, MAY FLOWER, STAR GRASS,
PIXIES, PISKEYS, THUNDER FLOWER

Height 15–60cm/6–24in ✸ April–June

Stellaria holostea
L *stellaria*, star; Gk *holo*, whole; *ostea*, bones

A weak straggly perennial often found in
groups in hedgerows and woods. Long, square,
hairy stems bear narrow stalkless leaves,
greyish and rough-edged. Deeply cleft 5-
petalled flowers are borne in loose clusters on
individual stalks. Sepals are shorter than the
petals.

As name suggests, once used in healing
bone fractures. Gerard said: 'drink it in wine
with the power of acorns against the pain in
the side, stitches and such-like'. Superstition
bestowed it with catastrophic properties –
picking it was supposed to provoke
thunderstorms, invite snake bites or
even bewitchment.

VIOLET, DAME'S

MOTHER OF EVENING, SWEET ROCKET,
VESPER FLOWER

Height 60–90cm/24–36in ❀ **May–August**

Hesperis matronalis
Gk *hespera*, evening (when scented);
L *matronalis*, of matrons

A hairy biennial or perennial with erect
unbranched stems with short-stalked toothed
and lance-shaped leaves. Flowers rather like
Milkmaids (*Northern Limestone*, page 78) borne
in loose clusters; purple, violet or white, and
very fragrant in evening. Mustard-like seeds
develop in slender upward-curving pods. A
sixteenth-century introduction from S Europe,
it soon became a cottage garden favourite.
Fairly common in N and S Cumbria and the
Eden Valley in damp lowland places; found
less often in Yorkshire woods and river banks.

Culpeper advised it for lung diseases,
asthma and chest infections. The acrid
leaves are eaten like cress in salads.

WATER CROWFOOT, POND

Height 5–15cm/1–3in ❀ **May–August**

Ranunculus peltatus
L *rana*, frogs (where they live); *peltatus*,
shield-shaped

An aquatic perennial with its roots in stream
or pond mud. Has branching, fine green
submerged leaves, and 3–7 lobed and notched
kidney-shaped or rounded aerial leaves. 5-
petalled white flowers with yellow centres are
raised above the water on individual erect
stems. Water-borne seeds developed in pear-
shaped capsules. Has the largest Water
Crowfoot flowers.

No specific medicinal or culinary uses.

WATER DROPWORT, HEMLOCK
DEAD TONGUE (N ENGLAND),
COWBANE (YORKSHIRE)

Height 60–120cm/24–48in ❀ June–August

Oenanthe crocata
L *oenanthe*, wine-fragrant; *crocata*, citron-
yellow (dye)

A sturdy, hairless, POISONOUS perennial
with large tubers attached by thin root stems
or 'drops'. Hollow upright stems are grooved
and stout. Glossy triangular leaves with oval
lobed and toothed leaflets, the leaf stalks
forming a sheath round the stem. Large
roundish umbrellas of clusters of small white
flowers stand erect above the stem. Up to 40
cylindrical seeds on separate short branches.
Plant smells of Parsley.
   The most deadly of British plants – cattle
and horses killed by eating dredged-up tubers.
Once used to kill rats and moles, and many
records of human fatalities. In Cumbria
it was used as a poultice on horses with galls.

WATER LILY, WHITE
WATERBELLS (N ENGLAND)

Surface flowering ❀ June–September

Nymphaea alba
L Nymphaea, classical water nymph;
alba, white

An aquatic perennial rising from a stout
rhizome. All leaves float on surface – almost
circular, green above, reddish below. Large
white flowers, up to 25 petals with yellow
stamens in middle, held erect above surface.
They open around noon and close in the
evening. Spongy globular fruits are green and
warty, up to 4cm/1½in in diameter.
   Seldom used medicinally, but has been
used for skin blemishes, baldness, bleeding,
dysentery, leucorrhoea, agues and pains. A
vaginal injection is reputed to cure uterine
cancer. The stems were once eaten as a
delicacy. For poets they were a symbol of
purity of heart.

WATERCRESS

WELL-KERSE (NORTHUMBERLAND)

Height 10–38cm/4–15in ❀ June–October

Nasturtium officinale
L *nasus-tortus*, twisted nose (refers to smell
of leaves); *officinale*, apothecary's herb
OE *wielle-cirse*, stream cress

A hairless, creeping, aquatic, winter-green
perennial with often-rooting hollow root
stems. Surface stems bear stalked leaves made
up of 5–11 pointed oval leaflets. 4-petalled
white flowers borne on loose spikes. Netted
seeds in 2 rows in cylindrical pods.

Rich in vitamin C, it was eaten raw or
boiled to prevent scurvy. Also has many
minerals, especially iodine, iron and
phosphorous. A blood cleanser, spring tonic,
diuretic and detoxifier, improving appetite
and relieving indigestion. Used in some
proprietary medicines. Culpeper said that
bruised leaves free the face from spots and
blemishes.

WINTERGREEN, ROUND-LEAVED

FALSE WINTERGREEN, BRITISH WINTERGREEN

Height 10–20cm/4–8in ❀ July–September

Pyrola rotundifolia ssp *maritima*
L *pyrola*, diminutive of *pyrus*, pear, *rotundifolia*,
round-leaved; ssp, subspecies

An evergreen perennial with a branching,
creeping rootstock. Bears a rosette of glossy,
dark green, round, toothed, long-stalked
leaves. A tall stem bears white, 5-petalled,
bell-shaped flowers rather like Lily of the
Valley, with short stalks and S-shaped styles.
Fruits in a capsule retaining style. A rare plant
of dune slacks, mainly in SW Cumbria,
including Walney Island.

Leaves diuretic and disinfectant. Decoction
used for dropsy, cystitis, rheumatics, diabetes
and urinary infection. Used by cosmetics
industry for its scent and flavour. Wintergreen
oil once used as an antiseptic, an ingredient of
embrocation, also a flavouring for sweets and
chewing gum.

ASTER, SEA

STARWORT

Height 15–60cm/6–24in ❀ July–October

Aster tripolium
L *aster*, star; *tripolium*, three-veined (of leaves)

A hairless perennial or annual with stout, often reddish stems and fleshy, green, clasping, lance-shaped leaves, with prominent midribs, which secrete fresh water to combat inundation by salt water. Daisy-like flowers with a central cluster of yellow florets and purplish blue rays are borne on separate stems in a loose cluster.

John Gerard (1597) said: 'the leaves of Aster or Inguinalis applied to botches and bewbones [groin swellings] which for the most part happen in Inguine, i.e. the flanke or share, do mightily maturate them, whereof this herb tooke the name of Inguinalis. The floures are good to be given unto children against the Squinancy and Falling Sicknesse.'

COMFREY

KNITBONE, BONESET

Height 25–120cm/10–48in ❀ May–October

Symphytum officinale
Gk *symphysis*, growing together; *phyton*, plants
Comfrey from L *confervere*, to grow together

An upright hairy perennial herb. Its tall branched stem is winged and bears large, hairy, broad, lance-shaped leaves right up the stem. Small coiled clusters of nodding bell-shaped flowers in white, cream, purple or pink droop from stem- sides and heads. Fruits are glossy black nutlets.

Young shoots are used in salads, soups, stews or like asparagus. Much used in proprietary medicines against flebitis, eczema, mastitis, haematoma, ulcers and gastritis. The leaves make good poultices or fomentations against sprains and bruises, cuts, boils and gangrenous ulcers. Roots mixed with Dandelion and Chicory make a tolerable coffee.

FIGWORT

THROATWORT, FIDDLE (YORKSHIRE), STINKING
ROGER, DEILEN DDU (WALES, 'GOOD LEAF')

Height 60–90cm/24–36in ☀ June–August

Scrophularia nodosa
L *scrofulae*, swelling of neck glands;
nodosa, knobbly

A knobbly rhizome bears a solid, erect square
stem, with toothed pointed-oval leaves. The
flowers are in a leafy open cluster, small,
2-lipped, the upper purplish-brown, the lower
green. Oval fruits are pointed at the top.
Brown seeds are cylindrical. Likes damp
lowland soils in woods or scrub.

   Knobbly root suggested a cure for piles or
'fig'. Romans knew it as *Cervicaria* because it
healed neck swellings and tumours. In Middle
Ages it was a cure for scrofula. Leaves used
as poultices for skin diseases, sores, abscesses
and gangrene. Edible root fed the garrison of
Rochelle during siege by Cardinal Richelieu
in 1628.

FUMITORY

WAX DOLLS (NORTHUMBERLAND, YORKSHIRE)

Height 15–50cm/6–20in ☀ May–September

Fumaria officinalis
L *fumus*, smoky; *officinalis*, medicinal

A robust, hairless, scrambling annual. Deeply
cut pinnate leaves have slender bluish-green
leaflets. Erect spikes bear many flowers,
tubular with a short spur, waisted, pinkish-
purple tipped maroon. Small single globular
seeds on short stalks succeed up the stem. Pull
a root to release a gaseous smell like nitric
acid. Common in waste places.

   Long used in Europe and beyond as a
diuretic, a gentle laxative, a detoxifier, to treat
liver, gall bladder and skin conditions, and as
a lotion to cleanse flaking skin and pimples.
Still used in a number of proprietary
medicines. Popular in France and Germany
as a blood purifier.

HEARTSEASE

SEASIDE OR WILD PANSY, LOVE-IN-IDLENESS

Height 15–30cm/6–12in ✤ April–September

Viola tricolor
L *Viola*, plant name; *tricolor*, three-coloured

A variable or perennial. Leafy ribbed,
branching, ascending stems rise direct from
fibrous roots, no runners. Oval, blunt-toothed
leaves are borne above fishbone-like stipules,
the upper leaves more lance-shaped. Flowers
smaller than Mountain Pansy, under 2.5cm/
1in across, flat-faced, short-spurred, with
violet-blue or mixed with yellow and white,
sometimes all yellow petals, the lower petal
veined. Slim, pointed sepals cradle an ovoid
capsule of seeds.

Diuretic, good for rheumatism and cystitis.
Used for bronchitis, whooping cough and skin
conditions. Gerard used it for fits, convulsions
and ague. Leaves used as litmus to test for
acidity or alkalinity. Oberon's fairies used its
juice to induce love (*Midsummer Night's Dream*).

HEMP-NETTLE

Height 10–100cm/4–40in ✤ July–September

Galeopsis tetrahit
L *galeo*, helmet, or *gale*, weasel; *opsis*, face
(flower); Gk *tetrahit*, foetid

A very hairy annual of the Mint or Deadnettle
family. Upright, square, hairy stems are
swollen below leaf nodes with red-tipped hairs
on opposite sides, and bear opposite, hairy,
strongly toothed nettle-like leaves. Pale
pinkish-purple, sometimes white or pale
yellow tubular flowers with a helmet above an
unnotched, 3-lobed lower lip, borne in whorls.
Much visited by bumble bees. 4 seeds in a
capsule. A plant of cultivated land, verges,
scrub and woodland. As with Hemp
Agrimony, single leaflets resemble Indian
Hemp.

Can be used for bronchitis, whooping
cough and trachaeitis, but Downy Hemp-
nettle more effective.

HOUND'S TONGUE

Height 30–90cm/12–36in 🌸 June–August

Cynoglossum officinale
Gk *kyon*, dog; L *glossum*, tongue (leaf shape);
officinale, medicinal herb

Branched, fleshy rootstock rears erect stems
with untoothed, lance-shaped, greyish,
alternate leaves with soft hairs. Dull purple,
5-petalled, funnel-shaped flowers held in loose
spikes. A hairy cup with hooked spines bears
4 nutlets. The whole plant smells of mouse or
roasted peanut. A greyish hairy perennial of
sandy places, common on Walney Island.

  Culpeper said leaves cured mad dog bites,
falling hair, burns and scalds; roots helped
lung and blood conditions or, baked, were
used as proprietary medicines for piles. Used in
proprietary medicines for piles, phlebitis,
eczema, mastitis, haematoma and gastritis.
Young shoots eaten like asparagus, young
leaves as a vegetable or in soups and stews.

LAVENDER, SEA

Height 20–35cm/8–14in 🌸 July–October

Limonium vulgare
Gk *leimon*, meadow; L *vulgare*, common

A much-branched hairless perennial of middle
salt marsh that extends into large colonies
reminiscent of pale heather moors. A basal
rosette of broad long-stalked, strongly veined,
spoon-shaped leaves give rise to pale green,
smooth, leafless and spreading rounded stems.
Crowded lavender flowers are held in flat-
topped, one-sided spikes. Single seeds held in
calices. The taller Lax-Flowered Sea Lavender,
Limonium humile, with squarer stems, is found
alongside it on the landward side of North
Walney Island.

  Gerard says that the seeds beaten into
powder and drunk with wine help the colic.
The flowers are often sold as everlastings.

LOOSESTRIFE, PURPLE

RED SALLY

Height 60–120cm/24–48in ✤ June–August

Lythrum salicaria
Gk *lythron*, blood; L *salicaria*, like salix (willow)

An erect perennial with a stout 4-sided hairy stem. Lower leaves, unstalked, in whorls of 3; upper leaves untoothed, lance-shaped, in opposite pairs like Sallow. Flowers are borne in whorls of 6 above small leaf-like bracts; reddish-purple, 6-petalled, and forming slender spikes at stem top. Oval capsule bears seeds. Introduced as an ornamental plant to the USA in the early nineteenth century, it has invaded wetlands in 48 states displacing native species, endangering dependent wildlife, and costing about $45 million a year to control.

Culpeper (1654) recommended it for eye complaints, for intermenstrual bleeding and to poultice wounds. In Ireland an infusion is used for diarrhoea and dysentery. The juice, rich in tannins, is an alternative to oak bark.

MARJORAM

WILD MARJORAM

Height 20–40cm/12–24in ✤ July–September

Origanum vulgare
Gk *oros*, mountain; *ganos*, joy; L *vulgare*, common or wild

A tufted hairy perennial with branching upright stems. Short-stalked, oval lance-shaped leaves in opposite pairs. Small bunched heads of 2-lipped purplish flowers borne above purplish bracts. The flowers have a notched upper, and a 3-lobed lower lip. Fruits are 4 nutlets in a cup of short pointed sepals.

Antibacterial, anti-fungal and antiseptic. Contains a volatile oil. Essences are good for coughs and breathing problems. Marjoram tea helps indigestion, earache, coughs, dropsy and bladder troubles. Diluted oil can be rubbed into aching teeth and joints. Perfume used in cosmetics. Symbolises happiness: young couples were crowned with Marjoram garlands in Greece and Rome.

MILKWORT, SEA

Height 10–30cm/4–12in ❀ May–September

Glaux maritima
Gk *glaux*, bluish-green (leaf colour);
L *maritima*, seaside

A low, creeping, mat-forming perennial of
sea shore, shingle and salt marsh. Prostrate,
rooting stems bear fleshy, stalkless, pointed
oval leaves in opposite pairs. Pink stalkless
flowers grow singly from leaf axils. Flowers
have no petals, only pink sepals. Fruits are
globular capsules that burst when ripe to
disperse seeds. The leaves store a reservoir
of water and reduce water evaporation,
reinforced by the plant's compact growth
form.

A member of the Primrose family with
similar but less potent medicinal values.
Its main use was the making of 'capers' by
pickling the new seed capsules.

MINT, WATER

HORSEMINT (N ENGLAND)

Height 15–60cm/6–24in ❀ July–October

Mentha aquatica
L *mentha*, mint, *aquatica*, of water

A perennial with a creeping, frequently
rooting, slender rootstock. Stiff, often reddish,
stems bear pairs of opposite, short-stalked,
pointed-oval, toothed, hairy leaves. Dense
clusters or whorls of lilac-coloured flowers
occur at base of upper leaves.

A strewing herb. Ancient Greeks used it in
bath water. In UK it was used for its cleansing,
refreshing, masking properties. Used against
diarrhoea and menstrual discharges. Mint tea
aids digestion; taken hot, it helps with heavy
colds by inducing perspiration. Used to flavour
gargles, mouthwashes and drinks.

NIGHTSHADE, WOODY

BITTERSWEET (CUMBERLAND, NORTHUMBERLAND), FELONWOOD (AGAINST FELONS, I.E. WHITLOWS)

Stems creep 20–300cm/12–80in   ❀ June–September

Solanum dulcamara
L *solanum*, large genus including potato, from *solor*, to ease; *dulcis*, sweet; *amarus*, bitter

A scrambling hairy perennial with woody stems. Leaves are stalked, oval- pointed with 2 narrow lobes at the base. Flowers in loose, drooping clusters, have 5 swept-back purple petals with yellow anthers in a cone shape. Green egg-shaped berries turn from green to yellow to red as they ripen. Many seeds in each berry.

Contains solanine, a narcotic alkaloid that tastes sweet, then bitter. Essence relieves spasms and epilepsy. Proprietary medicines use it against skin diseases, and rheumatic and blood disorders. Overdose can lead to paralysis of the tongue and finally loss of speech. Berries are POISONOUS.

ROCKET, SEA

RED BUNNY, PURPLE SEA ROCKET

Height 15–30cm/6–12in   ❀ June–August

Cakile maritima
Arab *Cakile*, plant name; L *maritima*, seaside

A succulent shoreline plant, untidy with fleshy, lobed, shiny leaves. 4-petalled lilac flowers are borne in loose terminal clusters. Stalked, stubby, waisted pods carry 2 smooth seeds. Common along the Cumbrian coast.

Culpeper describes its 'hot nature and bitterish taste that cleans the lungs of phlegm, helps breathing difficulties, is used as an emetic and helps jaundice and dropsy'. Anti-scorbutic, it is useful for scurvy, lymphatic disturbances and post-malarial sickness. For herbal uses it is most important not to confuse it with the safer Dame's Violet (*Hesperis matronalis*).

VETCH

FITCHES (CUMBERLAND,YORKSHIRE), COMMON
VETCH, LINTS (YORKSHIRE), TARE (YORKSHIRE)

Height 15–120cm/12–36in   ❀ June–September

Vicia sativa
L *vicia*, vetch; *sativa*, cultivated

A slightly hairy scrambling annual. Straggly
stems bear leaves with 4–8 opposite pairs of
lance-shaped leaflets and a tendril, often
branched, at the tips. Purple pea flowers,
solitary or in pairs, borne on short stalks up
the stem, their wings of a darker purple.
Smooth pods bearing 4–12 seeds have a long
beak. A fodder crop introduced in ancient
times from Western Asia, it is now ubiquitous
throughout the region, and common on
Walney Island.

VETCH, BITTER

HORSE-PEASE (CUMBERLAND),
PEASLING (YORKSHIRE)

Height 15–40cm/6–16in   ❀ April- July

Lathyrus montanus
Gk *lathyrus*, pea; L *montanus*, of the mountains

A delicate erect perennial with a creeping
rootstock. The hairless stem is round with 2
opposite ridges, and bears leaves consisting
of 2–4 opposite leaflets, lance-shaped with a
short point at the tip. Tall loose upright flower
stems bear 2–6 purple pea flowers, crimson
and turning bluish. Hairless pale brown pods
with beaked tips have up to 6 seeds.
   Recognised by William Turner in 1548,
when the tuberous rhizomes were dug up and
eaten. Gerard said they were harder to digest
than turnips or parsnips when boiled, but 'not
so windie'. They taste rather like chestnuts,
and on Colonsay were used to flavour whisky.
Similar to the Hairy Tare referred to in
Matthew XIII:30. An animal fodder crop.

VETCH, BUSH

CROW PEAS (CUMBERLAND)

Height 30–100cm/12–40in ✿ April–October

Vicia sepium
L *vicia*, vetch; *sepium*, of hedges

A hairy scrambling perennial. Ridged stems
bear downy leaves of 5–8 pairs of ovate leaflets
with terminal points, the whole leaf tipped
with branching support-seeking tendrils.
Purplish-blue pea flowers are borne in clusters
of 2–6. Seeds held in hairless pods tapering to
a beak turn black before seeds are ejected.
Called 'bush' not because it is one but because
it scrambles for support up through shrubs and
other plants. Widespread in hedges and scrub,
and very attractive to bumble bees.

    Although related to the Broad Bean it has
no culinary use, but was once fed to cattle.

VETCH, TUFTED

HUGGABACK (CUMBERLAND), MOUSE PEASE
(NORTHUMBERLAND), FINGERS AND THUMBS
(SOMERSET)

Height 60–200cm/24–80in ✿ June–August

Vicia cracca
L *vicia*, vetch; *cracca*, Pliny's name for vetch

A downy clambering perennial of hedge,
scrub, pasture and woodland edge. Ridged
stems bear leaves of 12–24 opposite, lance-
shaped leaflets with a tendril at the tip. Spikes
of up to 40 blue-purple pea flowers hang one-
sided on long erect stalks. Smooth brown pods
contain seeds. Pods end in a nail or claw,
giving the Somerset name of Fingers and
Thumbs. Common throughout the area
below 500m/1640ft.

    No known domestic use except as animal
fodder.

WOUNDWORT, HEDGE

ALL-HEAL, CLOWN'S WOUNDWORT

Height 30–90cm/12–36in ❀ June–September

Stachys sylvatica
Gk *stachys*, spike; L *sylvatica*, of woods

A strong-smelling creeping perennial. Hairy, upright, many-branched stems bear long-stalked, toothed, hairy heart-shaped leaves in opposite pairs. Loose spikes of flowers are borne in whorls, dark red-purple with tiny bracts below. Upper petals form hoods, lower have a white marked lobed lip. Hairy sepal tube holds seeds.

Effective in staunching wounds and applied as a poultice to remove warts and swellings around the head. The distilled juices of the flowers were used 'to make the heart merry, to make a good colour in the face, and make the vitall spirits more fresh and lively'. It produces a yellow dye. It is eaten by sheep and goats, but is shunned by cattle and pigs.

BALSAM, HIMALAYAN

INDIAN BALSAM, POLICEMAN'S HELMET,
NUNS, JUMPING JACK

Height 100–200cm/40–80in ❀ July–October

Impatiens glandulifera
L *impatiens*, from explosive seed release;
glandulifera, with glands

A fragile annual with ribbed, often reddish
stems. Leaves are in whorls of 3, pointed and
edged with short red teeth. Large reddish-
purple flowers are held on individual stalks in
small groups, spotted inside and with a sickly
scent. The name Policeman's Helmet is a good
description. Seeds are borne in exploding
narrow club-shaped capsules. Common in
South Lakeland in particular. A naturalised
Himalayan introduction, it grows to
300cm/10ft in its natural habitat.

Medical use, if any, is unknown. In the
Far East an extract is used as a nail varnish.

BINDWEED, SEA

SCAMMONY

Height 15–30cm/6–12in ❀ June–August

Calystegia soldanella
Gk *calyx*, cup; *stega*, covering; L *soldo*, round
coin; *anella*, small

A sprawling perennial with a spreading root
system. Hairless stems that seldom twist and
never climb bear long-stalked, fleshy, kidney-
shaped leaves. Red veined 5-bracted cradles
hold pink-striped white 5-petalled flowers in
a trumpet shape, 3–5cm/1–2in across.

Gerard says: 'very dangerous either if too
great a quantitie be taken or given without
correction or taken at the hands of some
runnagat physick-monger, quick salver, old
women leeches, and such like abusers of
physick and deceivers of people. The use of
Scammony I commit to the learned, unto
whom it especially and only belongeth, who
can very carefully and curiously use the same.'

GERANIUM, WALNEY

Height 5–20cm/2–8in ✿ July–August

Geranium sanguineum var. *Lancastriense*
Gk *geranos*, crane; L *sanguineum*, bloody;
Lancastriense, Lancastrian (until 1974
Walney Island was in Lancashire)

A creeping hairy perennial with leaves deeply
divided into 5 or 7 lobes. 5 slightly notched
pale pink-petalled flowers have distinctive
purplish veins. They grow alongside Bloody
Cranesbills which they closely resemble in all
ways except in colour. Typical Cranesbill fruit.
This is a very rare variant, declining in
population, found mainly on Walney Island,
but occasional rare specimens have been seen
further north up the Cumbian coast.

MALLOW

BILLY BUTTONS, PANCAKE PLANT,
CHEESE FLOWER

Height 30–90cm/12–36in ✿ June–September

Malva sylvestris
L *malva*, mallow; *sylvestris*, woodland

A southern biennial, regionally fairly rare, of
the coastal plains. A thick, erect hairy stem
bears kidney- to round-shaped lobed toothed
leaves. Large 2.5–5cm/1–2in rose-pink flowers
borne in clusters have 5 narrow notched dark-
veined petals. Rounded fruits, referred to as
'cheeses', contain netted nutlet seeds.

    Although now considered to be inferior to
Marsh Mallow, the white root is used in the
treatment of gravel, irritations of the kidneys
and, ground into a poultice and applied hot, to
remove wasp and bee stings or inflammation.
Pliny advocated applying the leaves crushed
with nitre to draw out thorns and prickles.
Flowers boiled in oil and water make a
soothing gargle.

MINT, SPEAR-

GARDEN MINT, LAMB MINT

Height 30–60cm/12–24in ❀ July–October

Mentha spicata
L *mentha*, mint family; *spicata*, spiked

A common mint introduced by the Romans who used it extensively at home. Creeping rootstocks throw up square, erect stems bearing in opposite pairs unstalked, greyish, sharply toothed, shiny, lance-shaped leaves, aromatic. Stems, sometimes branched, headed by spikes (spears) of tiny pink- or white-lipped flowers in close whorls above leaf bracts. Diminutive brown seeds dispersed by gravity and wind.

For medicinal purposes Peppermint is preferred, but the taste of Spearmint is less strong, so it is used for children's remedies, especially against fevers and inflammatory diseases. Mainly used in cooking as a flavouring, and in Kendal Mint Cake.

ORCHID, BEE

Height 15–60cm/6–24in ❀ June–July

Ophrys apifera
Gk *ophrys*, orchid; L *apifera*, bee-bearing

A widespread British orchid, seen in damp slacks near the north tip of Walney Island. It grows from 2 globular tubers. A single flower stem bears oval grey-green leaves that persist all winter, wrapped round the stem, with narrower leaves above. 2–7 widely spaced flowers mimic the appearance of bumble bees to encourage bees for pollination. Spreading, large, green-veined pink petals surround smaller curled-up green petals. The lip is bag-shaped, red or purplish-brown, softly hairy with a red-brown throat. It has side lobes like small hairy cones behind the lip. Self-pollinating so the attempt at deception seems unnecessary!

Culpeper says that the roots were used 'to provoke lust, to kill worms in children, to aid conception and provide a starchy alternative to potatoes during famine'.

PURSLANE, PINK

CLAYTONIA

Height 15–38cm/6–15in ✿ **April–August**

Claytonia sibirica
After John Clayton (1686–1773), a British
botanist living in America; L *sibirica*, from
Siberia
Also known as M*ontia perfoliata*, after
Giuseppi Monti (1682–1760); L *perfoliata*,
with leaves joined around the stem
Purslane possibly a corruption of porcelain

A low fleshy annual, sometimes over-
wintering, of acid woodland. A low rosette
of waxy stalked leaves cradles a stem with
unstalked, opposite, pointed oval leaves.
5-petalled pink flowers with veined deeply
notched petals are held in a loose cluster. A
North American introduction that thrives in
damp acid lowlands, often colonising woods
and coppices.

It was once cultivated for its edible roots
and as a salad herb.

REST HARROW

CAMMOCKY, WILD LICORICE

Height 20–60cm/8–24in ✿ **July–September**

Oenonis repens
Gk *Oenonis*, plant name; L *repens*, creeping
Rest harrow because it arrests farmers' harrows

A perennial woody sub-shrub with trailing
stems rooting at intervals. Small toothed oval
or trefoil leaves have tiny leaf-like stipules at
the base clasping the stems. Pink pea-flowers
are borne up erect stems. Seeds are in ovoid
pods. Common round Cumbrian coast and
Eden Valley.

Mildly diuretic, purgative. Dried roots used
as an infusion against dropsy, kidney and
bladder inflammation, skin disorders,
rheumatism and arthritis. Children once
chewed the roots like licorice. The leaves give
off a goat-like smell, and cattle feeding off it
produce 'cammocky', tainted milk.

ROSE, DOG

BRIAR, ENGLISH ROSE

Height 90–270cm/36–108in ❀ June–July

Rosa canina
L *rosa*, rose; *canina*, dog (common or
worthless)

A tall deciduous shrub with arching green
woody stems covered with downward-hooked
thorns. Alternate hairless leaves are made up
of a larger terminal leaflet and 2–3 opposite
pairs of similar toothed leaflets. Pink or white
5-petalled flowers held in loose clusters of 2–5.
Fruit is a fleshy smooth egg-shaped 'hip' filled
with hairy seeds.

  The Greeks believed roots would cure mad
dog bites. Culpeper said the acidic hips
strengthened the stomach, cooled fevers and
were good for coughs and blood discharges.
All parts of the plant have uses, especially for
heart and digestive problems, kidney disorders
and venereal disease. Gerard recommended
the hips to eat with meat or desserts.

SCURVYGRASS, DANISH

IVY-LEAVED SCURVYGRASS, EARLY
SCURVYGRASS

Height 5–25cm/2–10in ❀ April–September

Cochlearia danica
L *cochlea*, small snail shell; *danica*, Danish

A diminutive annual often found in broad
mats in dune slacks, especially on Walney
Island. Long-stalked rounded to triangular
heart-shaped leaves below, upper leaves ivy-
shaped and lobed. Upright forked stem bears
small clusters of 4-petalled pink flowers. Oval
seeds in egg-shaped pods. Common round
coast, but currently colonising the M6 central
reservation in Cumbria and Lancashire.

  Culpeper writes: 'This plant possesses a
considerable degree of acrimony: it is anti-
scorbutic, and a powerful remedy in moist
asthma or scorbutic rheumatism'.

SPURREY, GREATER SAND-

Height 5–15cm/2–6in ❀ May–September

Spergularia media
L *spergularia*, plant name; *media*, middle

A sprawling, slender, hairless perennial
of muddy salt marsh. Reddish stems bear
whorls of succulent linear green leaves with
terminal and branching sparse flowerheads.
5 unnotched violet-pink petals, a little longer
than the sepals, have white centres. Seeds are
winged. The largest of a group of relatively
insignificant seaside plants, mainly of salt
marshes, to be found in several European
coastal regions. Common nationally, but rarer
in Cumbria, existing mainly in the extreme
north and south, including Walney Island
where similar but white Corn Spurrey
(*Spergula arvensis*) also occurs.

   The plant has been used for the treatment
of bladder diseases and cystitis.

STORKSBILL

Height 5–50cm/2–20in ❀ May–September

Erodium circutarium
Gk *erodium*, heron; L *circutarium*, round
(shape of fruit)

A variable, hairy perennial of dry sandy
grasslands. Erect or prostrate hairy stems bear
opposite pairs of divided, fern-like leaves,
hairy, sometimes with glands, and often
apparently encrusted in small sand grains.
Pink or white flowers with 5 petals and 5
sepals are borne in loose umbrellas. Long-
beaked seed pods like those of Herb Robert
split into 5 segments with a seed at the base,
twisting to anchor themselves into the
ground. Fairly common round the Cumbrian
coast and Eden Valley on sand and lime.

   A preparation of the whole plant was used
to stem uterine and other bleeding. Young
leaves added to salads, sauces, omelettes,
soups and sandwiches.

THRIFT

SEA PINK, MARSH DAISY (CUMBERLAND), SCAWFELL PINK (CUMBERLAND)

Height 5–22.5cm/2–9in ❀ May–August

Armeria maritima
L *Armeria*, plant name; *maritima*, near the sea

A tufted perennial of seaside and mountains. Long penetrating roots raise tight cushions of fleshy bluish-green linear grass-like leaves. Leafless downy upright stems bear tight terminal rosettes of honey-scented pink flowers with a collar of papery brown bracts. Almost everlasting.

No medicinal use. Culpeper says: 'It is a plant of Saturn, very astringent, but not often used'. Gerard says: 'Their use in Physicke as yet is not knowne, neither doth any seeke into the Nature thereof, but esteem them only for their beautie and pleasure'. Often grown in rockeries.

WILLOWHERB, BROAD-LEAVED

MOUNTAIN WILLOWHERB

Height 30–60cm/12–24in ❀ June–November

Epilobium montanum
Gk *epi*, upon; *lobos*, pod (flower is above pod); L *montanum*, of the mountains

A slightly hairy perennial, a common garden weed. A rounded upright stem bears short-stalked, opposite, toothed oval leaves. Solitary flowers rise from leaf joints each with 4 notched petals on the end of a long seed pod. Plumed seeds dispersed by wind. A common plant of wasteland and upland damp ghylls and gullies. Named because the leaves resemble those of the Willow.

Culpepper states: 'All the species of Willowherbs have the same virtues: they are under Saturn and are cooling and astringent. The root powdered and dried is good against haemorrhages; the fresh juice acts the same.'

WILLOWHERB, GREAT

CODLINS AND CREAM (CUMBERLAND,
YORKSHIRE), APPLE PIE (NORTHUMBERLAND,
YORKSHIRE), GREAT HAIRY WILLOWHERB

Height 80–152cm/32–60in ✽ July–September

Epilobium hirsutum
Gk *epi*, upon; *lobos*, pod; L *hirsutum*, hairy

A hairy perennial, the biggest and largest-
flowered Willowherb. Erect hairy stems bear
opposite, stalkless, hairy, lance-shaped,
toothed leaves, half-clasping the stems.
Flowers of 4 notched purplish-pink petals are
held in a leafy spike. Seeds in a long slender
capsule. Common in damp areas near water.

Of limited medicinal value but made into
tea in Russia. The name Codlins and Cream
comes from the red and white flowers, codlins
being red cooking apples

CAMPION, RED

WAKE ROBIN (YORKSHIRE), BACHELORS'
BUTTONS, MARY JANES (CUMBERLAND),
MOTHER DIE

Height 30–90cm/12–36in ❀ **May–November**

Silene dioica
Gk *silene*, name of similar plant after Silenus,
a merry drunken woodland god; L *dioica*,
divided (M and F on separate stems)

A hardy perennial with a creeping stock, often
in clumps. Hairy, very upright, flowering stems
bear pointed oval leaves, stalked at base,
unstalked and opposite up the stem. Deeply
divided 5-petalled flowers are unscented. Sepals
are joined to form a sticky tube. Fruits in
capsules with 10 teeth rolled back when ripe.

Culpeper used it for kidney stoppages, stones,
internal bleeding, cleaning old sores and
wounds, and in wine against scorpion stings,
snake bites and plague. In Wales, a plant of the
snake, devil, goblin and death; in the Isle of
Man, the fairies' flower, not to be picked or else!

CLOVER, RED

COW GRASS (N ENGLAND),
CLAVER (N ENGLAND), HONEYSUCK,
SOUKIES (NORTHUMBERLAND, SCOTLAND)

Height 10–60cm/4–24in ❀ **May–September**

Trifolium pratense
L *tri*, three; *folium*, leaf; *pratense*, of meadows

A downy perennial of grassy places. Pointed
oval trefoil leaflets have a whitish V shape
across them. Flowers in dense heads above
2 leaves at head of stem. Dead flowers persist
(brown) to protect small seed pods.

Used for skin conditions, and as an
expectorant, a syrup for whooping cough and
a menopausal aid. Has a contraceptive effect
in sheep. Fixes nitrogen in soil. The flowers
make a pleasant wine. 3-leaved lucky, 4-leaved
very lucky, charm against witchcraft, enabling
people to see fairies and break their powers of
enchantment.

DEADNETTLE, RED

BAD MAN'S POSIES (YORKSHIRE,
NORTHUMBERLAND), DEVIL'S POSIES,
PURPLE ARCHANGEL

Height 10–45cm/4–18in ❀ March–December

Lamium purpurium
L *Lamium*, plant name; *purpurium*, dull
red-purple

A sprawling, downy annual with a pungent
smell if crushed. Squarish, often purplish stems
bear wrinkled, bluntly toothed, oval, heart-
shaped leaves with pointed tips in opposite
pairs on short stalks. Pinkish-purple 2-lipped
flowers, the upper lip a hood, the lower 2-
lobed, are borne in leafy clusters up the stem.
Pointed sepals form a cup for 4 nutlet seeds.

 Bruised leaves applied to wounds. Herb tea
from leaves eases kidney problems and purifies
blood. Has been used against scrofula and the
boiled roots in sweet milk to purge measles. If
boiled, it can be used as a pot herb or in pig
swill.

PIMPERNEL, SCARLET

POOR MAN'S WEATHERGLASS,
SHEPHERD'S WEATHER GLASS (YORKSHIRE)

Height 5–30cm/2–12in ❀ June–October

Anagallis arvensis
Gk *anagallis*, to laugh (after liver cure);
L *arvensis*, of cultivated fields

A slender creeping perennial with 4-angled
stems bearing opposite unstalked pointed-oval
shiny leaves with black glands on undersides.
Solitary 5-petalled red flowers rise from leaf
joints on slender stems. Seeds develop in a
globular capsule. Flowers open from 8 a.m.
until 3 p.m. No scent or nectar; seldom visited
by insects.

 Once used for gallstones, urinary infections,
epilepsy, rheumatism, mental problems,
toothache and snake bite. Not now used
except in homeopathy for skin eruptions,
warts, liver and gall bladder disorders. Leaves
can cause dermatitis. The Greeks thought it
eased melancholy.

ALKANET, GREEN

EVERGREEN ALKANET

Height 30–l00cm/12–40in ❀ May–August

Pentaglottis sempervirens
Gk *penta*, five; *glottis*, windpipe or tongue;
L *sempervirens*, evergreen
Arab Alkanet, from *al-henna*, henna,
shrub with roots yielding a red dye

A tufted bristly perennial with an upright
branched stem bearing hairy stalked oval
leaves. Upper leaves unstalked and paler
below. Flat white-eyed blue flowers with
5 petals borne in long coils that uncurl as
the flowers mature. Seeds are 4 nutlets with
raised edges.

   Medicinal use similar to Comfrey (both are
in the Borage family). It is commonly found
near habitations, where it was formerly
cultivated for medicinal uses. Used in
monastic times also as a red dye.

BUGLOSS

BUGLOSS, SMALL OR COMMON

Height 15–50cm/6–20in ❀ April–September

Anchusa arvensis
L *anchusa*, paint (dye from roots); *arvensis*,
of cultivated fields
Bugloss from Gk for bull's tongue.

An upright, bristly annual superficially like
Green Alkanet. Hairy, alternate, lance-shaped
leaves, irregularly toothed, often wavy at the
edges, lower ones stalked, upper clasping the
hairy stem. Almost stalkless flowers with 5
blue petals on kinked white tubes are borne
in forked terminal clusters. Seeds are 4 brown
nutlets in the sepal case. Found mainly on
Walney Island and Eden Valley.

   Probably has same medicinal properties
as Alkanet and Viper's Bugloss, but not
commonly used. Red dye from roots used on
wood to imitate rosewood; once used as rouge.

BUGLOSS, VIPER'S

Height 30–60cm/12–24in ❀ June–September

Echium vulgare
L *echis*, viper; *vulgare*, common

An upright bristly perennial of light dry soils. Speckled hairy stems have basal leaves like an ox tongue covered with white hairs and a prominent midriff. Flowers are borne in coiled sprays forming a prominent snake's-head-like spike. Flower buds are pink, blue when open, the sprays gradually uncoiling. Close up, individual flowers resemble gentians. Long pointed sepals nurture 4 angular nutlets.

Sweat inducing and diuretic, used since ancient Greek times to ease lumbago, increase mothers' milk, for coughs and chest conditions, and for skin complaints. The seeds resembling snake heads were thought to cure snake bites. Once believed effective against sadness and melancholy. Toxic alkaloids debar internal use.

CRANESBILL, MEADOW

BLUE BASINS

Height 30–76cm/12–30in ❀ June–September

Geranium pratense
Gk *geranos*, crane; L *pratense*, of meadows

A hairy perennial with reddish stems bearing long-stalked, deeply lobed and toothed leaves with leaf-like scales at the base. 5-petalled, unnotched, large blue flowers are borne in pairs at stem ends. Hairy beak-shaped seed heads bear several seeds that rise on fine coiled stems when ripe. Common on roadsides and riversides, once in hay meadows. As with all the geranium family, the leaves are a favourite part of the diet of the roe deer.

Culpeper does not mention it and Gerard refers only to Dove's Foot Cranesbill so presumably it was of little or no medicinal value.

FORGET-ME-NOT

SCORPION GRASS, LOVE-ME (YORKSHIRE),
COMMON OR FIELD FORGET-ME-NOT

Height 7.5–30cm/3–13in ❀ **April–December**

Myosotis arvensis
Gk *mus*, mouse; *otos*, ears (leaf shape);
L *arvensis*, of fields

A soft hairy annual or biennial branched at
the base. A rosette of hairy pointed-oblong
stalked leaves cradles an upright stem with
smaller unstalked leaves and a terminal loose
spike or spikes of saucer-shaped, yellow-eyed,
blue flowers opening progressively upwards.
Fruits are dark brownish-black nutlets on
longish stalks in a hairy sepal cup.

Used for lung ailments and to harden steel.
A symbol of love. A German tale tells how a
knight picked these flowers for his lady as they
walked by a river. He slipped, fell in and was
drowned, but not before throwing the flowers
to his lady crying, 'Vergisz mein nicht!'
(Forget me not!)

HOLLY, SEA

ERINGO, WATLING STREET THISTLE

Height 15–60cm/6–24in ❀ **July–August**

Eryngium maritimum
Gk *eruggarein*, to eructate or belch (used for
flatulence); L *maritimum*, seaside

A rigid tufted perennial with a creeping
rootstock giving rise to a number of rigid erect
stems bearing spiky, leathery, blue-green,
holly-like leaves. The flower is a round head
of blue florets skirted with spiny bracts in
groups at stem top. Oval fruits are covered
with hooked hairs. Common on sandy and
shingle beaches of W Cumbria.

Recommended by Culpeper for liver
ailments, kidney stones, venereal disease,
scrofula, snake bites, wounds and ear
infections. Gerard said: 'The roots restore
natural moisture to old people withered with
age, amending the defects of nature in the
younger.' The candied roots, 'eringoes', were
thought aphrodisiac, especially for the elderly.

SCABIOUS, FIELD

BLUE BUTTONS (CUMBERLAND), MEADOW
SCABIOUS, GIPSY ROSE (YORKSHIRE),
LADY'S PIN CUSHION

Height 25–100cm/10–40in ❀ July–September

Knautia arvensis
After Dr Knaut, a seventeenth-century botanist
from Saxony; L *arvensis*, field

A tall hairy perennial with notched, undivided
lance-shaped basal leaves, its upper leaves much
divided like a fish-bone and hairy. Blue-mauve
flowers held in a pincushion of up to 50 florets,
the outer ones larger and rayed. Seeds crowned
with bristles and 16 tiny purple sepals. Grows in
low dry areas; becoming fairly uncommon.

A long-used cure for scabies (hence its
common name), other skin diseases and plague.
Infusions taken for purifying the blood, and
applied to cuts, burns and bruises. Decoction
or ointment made from roots cured sores,
eruptions and other skin defects. Gipsies use
it to strengthen the lungs and for pleurisy.

SOW-THISTLE, BLUE

Height 60–150cm/24–60in ❀ July–September

Cicerbita macrophylla
L *cicerbita* from Ital name for sow-thistles;
macrophylla, large-leaved

A tall patch-forming perennial now spreading
throughout the region on roadsides and waste
ground. Tall upright stems bear bristly leaves,
narrow and winged for two-thirds up then
swelling into a large heart-shaped lobe. Broad
loose clusters of pale violet-blue flowers, similar
to Chicory, crown the stems. Fruits hairless,
slightly winged. Multiplies mainly by creeping
rhizomes. Introduced from the Ural Mountains
of Russia, it is a different species from the
Alpine Sow-Thistle of the Caucasus and
Europe.

Culpeper held it in high regard for treating
urinary gravel, haemorrhoids, gout and
deafness. Like all the Sow-Thistles, which
carry a milky latex, it has been used on the
Continent in salads and cooked like spinach.

SPEEDWELL, THYME-LEAVED

THYME SPEEDWELL

Height 5–25cm/2–10in ❀ April–October

Veronica serpyllifolia
After St Veronica who wiped the face of Christ
while he carried the cross; L *serpens*, creeping;
folia, leaves

A slightly downy creeping perennial, rooting
frequently. Shiny, short-stalked, untoothed,
oval leaves grow in opposite pairs. Pale blue
4-petalled flowers borne in leafy terminal
spikes. Seed capsule heart-shaped and hairy.

Culpeper says: 'Venus governs this plant,
and it is among the vulnerary plants, used both
inwardly and outwardly; it is also pectoral and
good for coughs and consumptions; the stone
and the strangury, and against pestilential
fevers.' The name Speedwell implies that it is
quick to heal, or it may be from the good-luck
buttonhole given in Ireland to those about to
set off on a journey.

BEET, SEA

WHITE BEET, SEA SPINACH, WILD SPINACH

Height 30–60cm/12–24in ⚜ June–September

Beta vulgaris ssp *maritima*
L *beta*, beetroot; *maritima*, seaside;
ssp, sub-species

A sprawling, hairless, sometimes red-ringed perennial with a hard long root. Sprawling and erect stems bear shiny, leathery, untoothed, heart-shaped leaves. Green flowers with prominent yellow stamens and styles borne in leafy spikes. Seeds in clusters of small globular capsules. Wind pollinated.

Culpeper says: 'It doth loosen the belly, and is of a cleansing, digesting quality and provoketh urine . . . is good for all weals, pustules, blisters and blains in the skin . . .' The leaves can be used like spinach, but Gerard says that 'it nourisheth little or nothing, and is not as wholesome as lettuce'.

BRYONY, BLACK

MANDRAKE (YORKSHIRE)

Height 180–360cm/72–144in ⚜ May–July

Tamus communis
Gk *Tamus*, name for similar plant;
L *communis*, common
Bryony from Gk *bruonia*, to swell

A hairless, perennial climbing hedgerow plant rising from a long black unbranched tuber. Slender twining stems, unbranched, bear heart-shaped leaves but no tendrils. Shiny leaves arranged spirally. Tiny yellow-green flowers in small clusters from leaf-axils. Fruit is a shiny scarlet berry.

Culpeper said: 'a furious Martial plant. The root purgeth the belly with great violence, troubling the stomach and burning the liver.' Dioscorides used it to remove freckles and spots. In France it was 'the herb for battered wives'. Herbalists now use it for rheumatic conditions, but it can cause blisters.

DOCK, BROAD

WAYSIDE DOCK, BUTTER DOCK, ROUND-
LEAVED DOCK, MONK'S RHUBARB

Height 30–90cm/12–36in ✿ June–October

Rumex obtusifolia
L *rumex*, name for sorrels; *obtusifolia*,
blunt-leaved

A sturdy tap-rooted perennial. Basal leaves
broad and heart-shaped at base with hairy
veins below. Upper leaves broad and lance-
shaped with wavy, not curled edges. Flowers
are borne in whorls in spreading branches up
a spike, the long-toothed petals covering the
fruits, which are triangular, toothed, with one
red valve bigger than the others. The sturdiest
of common docks. A scheduled injurious
weed, difficult to eradicate.

Leaves used for burns, scalds, blisters and
nettle stings. Root tea used to treat boils.
Wrapping butter in its leaves gave it the
name Butter Dock.

GOOD KING HENRY

MERCURY (CUMBERLAND, YORKSHIRE),
SMEARWORT

Height 30–60cm/12–24in ✿ May–August

Chenopodium bonus-henricus
Gk *chen*, goose; *podion*, foot; L *bonus-henricus*
after the German Guter Heinrich, Good
Henry, a goblin similar to Robin Goodfellow,
with knowledge of healing plants

The only perennial Goosefoot. Tall, rigid,
erect, hollow stems bear triangular, almost
arrow-shaped, wavy-edged leaves, mealy at
first then dull green. A narrow pyramidal
terminal spike, almost leafless, bears
insignificant greenish flowers. Bladder-like
pod contains one seed.

Leaf poultices were used to clean and heal
chronic sores, hence the name Smearwort. No
longer considered to be of any medicinal use.
Young leaves, rich in iron, can be used like
spinach, young shoots like asparagus.

NAIAD, SLENDER

Height 10–20cm/4–8in ❀ **August–September**

Najas flexilis
Gk *najas* or L *naias*, water nymph, believed to
live in and give life to rivers, springs and lakes;
L *flexilis*, flexible

A rare slender and protected perennial of
Lakeland tarns and Scottish and W Ireland
ponds and lochs. The greater part submerged,
fine stems bear thin, linear, toothed, grass-like
leaves in threes or opposite pairs. Small
insignificant green flowers rise from leaf axils,
separate male and female on same plant.
Minute seeds are water-borne. Known to exist
in Elterwater (Walk 4) and Long Moss, Torver
Back Common (Walk 2).
　　No known medicinal or culinary uses.

PEARLWORT, MOSSY

PROCUMBENT PEARLWORT, PEARLWORT

Height 2.5–15cm/1–6in ❀ **April–October**

Sagina procumbens
L *sagina*, fodder; *procumbens*, prostrate

A low spreading mat-forming perennial of
bare stony places or garden paths. Long
slender stalks bear narrow, opposite, lance-
shaped leaves each ending in a tiny bristle.
Greenish 4-petalled flowers droop after
flowering then become erect when fruit
ripens. Like a moss.
　　Of superstitious rather than medicinal
qualities. Believed to have been the first plant
Christ stood on on earth, or when he rose
from the dead. In Scotland, having been
blessed by Christ, St Bride and St Columba,
it was hung over doors against evil spirits. An
infusion was used to attract a maiden's lover,
and if she kissed the plant he would be hers
for ever.

PONDWEED, BOG

Surface hugging ❀ May–September

Potamogeton polygoniferous
Gk *potamus*, river; *geiton*, neighbour; *poly*,
many; *goni*, angled; L *folius*, leaved

An aquatic perennial of acid waters. Long-stemmed leaves rise to the surface from a creeping rhizome in the bottom mud. Floating pointed-oval alternate leaves lack the flexible stem joints that typify Broad-Leaved Pondweed. A few lance-shaped submerged leaves. Stalked dense spikes of green flowers, tinged red like the leaves, turn brown to resemble Plantain heads. Fruits turn reddish-brown. Sometimes grows in Sphagnum moss. The commonest pondweed in lakes, tarns and ditches on acid soils in the Lakes and Dales.

SALTWORT

PRICKLY GLASSWORT, PRICKLY SALTWORT

Height 10–60cm/4–24in ❀ July–September

Salsola kali
L *sal*, salt; Arab *al-qili*, ashes of Saltwort
(cf alkali)

A stiff, semi-recumbent, hairy annual with a thick grey-green stem, often striped pink, bearing stubby, fleshy, bluish-green leaves, pointed at the tips. Solitary inconspicuous green flowers are borne up the stem in tufts of leaf-like bracts. The flower-like fruits are cradled by persistent petals and sepals.

The whole plant, rich in soda, was burnt to get soda-ash; fused with sand, this produced a poor-quality glass. Used in biblical times to make glass and soap. As a salad plant it can be eaten raw, cooked like spinach, or mixed with other vegetables. Once pickled to accompany meat dishes.

SORREL

SOUR DOCK, VINEGAR LEAVES (LANCASHIRE),
GREEN SAUCE (LANCASHIRE, YORKSHIRE)

Height 15–60cm/6–24in ❀ May–August

Rumex acetosa
L *Rumex*, plant name; *acetosa*, acidic leaves

A perennial with a deep slender tap root.
Long-stalked arrow-shaped leaves arranged
alternately up an erect stem, their basal lobes
pointing backwards. Branched upper stem bears
whorls of insignificant greenish flowers, male
and female on separate plants. After flowering
the petals curve inwards to protect the ovary,
and turn red giving the spike a red hue.

Diuretic, refrigerant, detoxicant, anti-
scorbutic. The juice takes rust marks out of
linen. Used to flavour salads and soups and to
flavour and tenderise cold meat. Leaves, pulped
and mixed with vinegar and sugar, make a green
sauce for fish. Boiled leaves (no water) served
with pork or goose instead of apple sauce.

SPURGE, PORTLAND

BROAD LEAVED SPURGE

Height 7.5–23cm/3–9in ❀ April–September

Euphorbia portlandica
After Euphorbus, physician to Juba, first-
century King of Mauretania; L *portlandica*,
from Portland

A short greyish biennial of sand dunes and
limestone cliffs. Erect stems, often red, bear
untoothed blunt-pointed oval leaves, leathery
with a pronounced midriff below. Pale
yellowish-green pointed oval bracts in
opposite pairs cradle similar coloured,
insignificant horned flowers. A capsule bears
pale grey seeds. Similar to Sea Spurge,
Euphorbia paralias, which has no red stems,
and has more leaves overlapping the stems.
Common on western sand dunes.

Culpeper writes: 'All the spurges purge
serious and choleric humours very violently,
and help the dropsy and inveterate asthma.'
Sap once used to burn off warts.

SPURGE, SEA

Height 15–24cm/6–10in ✤ June–October

Euphorbia paralias
L after Euphorbus (see Spurge, Portland);
paralis, on the beach

A grey, hairless, tufted perennial, taller than
Portland Spurge with robust upright stems,
not reddening. Broader, more numerous, greyer
leaves overlap and clasp the stem, the midrib
less prominent. Small yellowish-green flowers
with shorter horns, cradled by pointed-oval,
pale yellowish-green bracts are borne in
branching terminal candelabra. Wrinkled
capsules bear smooth pale grey seeds.
  Gerard writes: 'The juyce mixed with hony
causeth haire to fall from that place which is
anointed therewith, if it be done in the sun.
The juyce or milke is good to stop hollow teeth,
being put into them warily, so that you touch
neither the gums nor any of the other teeth in
the mouth with the said medicine. It killeth
fish, being mixed with any thing that they eat.'

TOWN HALL CLOCK

MOSCHATEL, MUSKWEED, MUSK RANUNCULUS

Height 10–15cm/4–6in ✤ April–May

Adoxa moschatellina
Gk *adoxa*, inglorious; L *moschata*, musky smell

A slender hairless perennial with long-stalked
leaves divided into 3, stalked, 3-lobed leaflets,
rather like a Wood Anemone. 5-faceted green
flowers held erect on slender stems with one
flower on each of 4 sides and one facing
upwards. Green fruits like tiny acorns. When
damp or at dusk it smells of musk. Widespread
on hedge banks at lower levels, but shy and
hard to spot. John Ray classified it among the
berry-bearing plants! Found in hedgerows all
over the region, prolific in Dentdale.

Opposite: River Wharfe in
Langstrothdale, Walk 11

WALKS

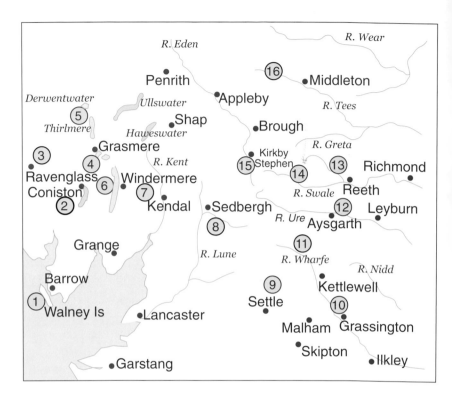

SYMBOLS USED IN THE MAPS

Road		▲	Hilltop
Track or bridleway		▲	Youth Hostel
River or beck		⬢	Viewpoint
Walking route		▬	Building
Wall or hedge		☩	Church or chapel
Railway		(P)	Parking
Upper Slopes Lower		(WC)	Toilets

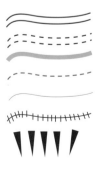

WALKS

		km	miles	hours
1	NORTH WALNEY ISLAND	8	5	1/2 DAY
2	TORVER TARNS & CONISTON WATER	8	5	2 1/2–3
3	EEL TARN, R. ESK & STANLEY FORCE	9	5 1/2	3–4
4	ELTERWATER & LITTLE LANGDALE	10	6 1/4	2 1/2–3 1/2
5	RIVER DERWENT & BORROWDALE	8	5	3–3 1/2
6A	CLAIFE TARNS & WINDERMERE	10.5	7	4–5 1/2
6B	CLAIFE TARNS & WINDERMERE	15	9 1/2	4–5 1/2
7	RIVER KENT & COCKSHOT WOOD	10	6 1/4	3–4
8	DENTDALE	10.5	6 1/2	3 1/2–4
9	RIVER RIBBLE & CATRIGG FORCE	7	4 1/2	2 1/2–3 1/2
10	MID WHARFEDALE & BURNSALL	11	7	3 1/2–4 1/2
11A	UPPER WHARFE & HUBBERHOLME	12	7 1/2	3 1/2–4 1/2
11B	UPPER WHARFE & HUBBERHOLME	8	5	3
12	RIVER BAIN & SEMERWATER	13	8	4–5
13	ARKLE BECK, SWALEDALE	6.5	4	2 1/2–3
14	UPPER SWALEDALE & KELD	9	6	3–3 1/2
15	RIVER EDEN & KIRKBY STEPHEN	7	4 1/2	2 1/2–3 1/2
16	RIVER TEES & HIGH FORCE	12	7 1/2	4–5

INTRODUCTION

The walks have been specially chosen to ensure the discovery of different species where they are to be seen, often in local abundance, however rare they may be nationally. All the flowers in this book are accompanied with simple non-technical descriptions, including size and preferred habitats; the flowering charts, specific to Northern England, should further assist in identification. As in Volume 1, *Limestone Flowers*, all the species are to be seen within two metres of public or permitted footpaths, thus eliminating any need to trespass to find them. On common land, such as Torver Common and Malham National Nature Reserve, access is unrestricted.

In addition, the routes selected offer picturesque landscapes, often from an elevated viewpoint, making them classic walks in their own right.

The original maps have been drawn to show only relevant landmarks and features, even down to field walls (thin black lines) in cases where finding the route might be difficult. Walking routes are indicated by dotted red lines, with red arrows to indicate preferred directions, but since all walks are circular they can be taken in the opposite direction, depending on weather conditions. Exposed upland paths, for example, should be done with a following wind, while strong headwinds need to be countered by sheltered valley or woodland paths.

The majority of the walks would be classified as easy. Times given are based on an average rate of two miles per hour, enough to allow for refreshment breaks and stops for detailed inspection of plants. Most of the maps have sufficient detail to enable the routes to be shortened or extended if desired.

The best footwear is boots or strong shoes with grooved soles, although for lower-level walks trainers or Wellingtons would suffice. Sudden changes of weather are possible at all times, so waterproof and windproof garments are recommended. Food is a personal consideration, but on a hot day water or soft drinks are essential, since beck water is often polluted by animals and should not be drunk.

In 1997 the Ordnance Survey issued a new series (NS) of Outdoor Leisure Maps that considerably extended the boundaries of the old series (OS). References are given to both.

Opposite: Marsh Marigolds (*Caltha palustris*; page 39)
at Upper Teesdale, Walk 16

NORTH WALNEY ISLAND SEASIDE PLANTS

Walney Island has been selected from a number of locations because of its wide diversity of maritime plant pecies and its ease of access. It typifies the coastal areas of most of the country as well as the entire Cumbrian coast.

The island is largely of glacial origin, consisting of sand, silt and boulder clay resting on Mercian mudstones. Interestingly, between here and St Bees Head the tidal drift is southwards, whereas elsewhere on the west coast it flows in a northward direction. On its western side, large shingle beds protect its great sand dunes from the prevailing westerly winds and tides.

LOOK OUT FOR

The more protected eastern shore owes its character more to the deposition of sands and silts by the twice-daily tidal flow, and consists of **salt marshes** that are inundated by spring tides.

Annual Seablite, Glasswort, Lax-Flowered Sea Lavender, Sea Aster, Sea Lavender, Sea Purslane, Sea Milkwort and Thrift.

To the west of the salt marshes lies **agricultural** ground largely grazed by sheep and bounded by hedges and ditches.

Angelica, Meadowsweet, Purple Loosestrife and Sneezewort.

Beyond the pastures and also grazed by island sheep are a few **acid heaths**, leached of minerals.

Bell Heather, Cross-leaved Heath, Ling, Marsh Cinquefoil, Sundew, Tormentil.

The spectacular **sand dunes** suffer constant erosion from wind, weather and human trampling.

Bloody Cranesbill, Burnet Rose, Carline Thistle, Coral Root Orchid, Heartsease, Lady's Bedstraw, Rest Harrow, Sea Spurge and Walney Geranium.

In the damp **dune slacks** you will find a wide range of flowers.

Autumnal Hawkbit, Bee Orchid, Goatsbeard, Haresfoot Clover, Lesser Hawkbit, Marsh Helleborine, Rough Hawkbit, Round-leaved Wintergreen, Sneezewort, Spotted Orchid, Sticky Groundsel, Strawberry Clover and Yellow Rattle.

In the past sand, and gravel have been reclaimed from Walney Island leaving large ponds where the rare Natterjack Toad breeds. The **pond margins** boast a wide variety of species.

Centaury, Dwarf Purple Orchid, Early Marsh Orchid, Gipsywort, Hemlock Water Dropwort, Hemp-Nettle, Hound's Tongue, Kidney Vetch, Lousewort, Marsh Bedstraw, Marsh Pennywort, Marsh Willowherb, Parsley Water Dropwort, Ragged Robin, Perennial Sow-Thistle, Seaside Centaury, Smooth Hawksbeard, Toadflax and Weld.

Buffeting the island from the often turbulent Irish Sea, the **shingle banks** of the western shoreline are colonised by hardy plants.

Common Orache, Frosted Orache, Grass-leaved Orache, Prickly Saltwort, Sea Bindweed, Sea Campion, Sea Holly, Sea Kale, Sea Mayweed, Sea Rocket, Sea Spurge and Yellow-Horned Poppy.

A visit is strongly recommended to the southern part of the island (SD215621), a reserve of the Cumbrian Wildlife Trust (a nominal entry fee is charged). Here are breeding colonies of gulls, terns, eider duck and many smaller species of birds. As well as many of the plants seen in the northern reserve, there are others specific to the area.

Black Nightshade, Bugloss, Corn Spurrey, Danish Scurvygrass, Fragrant Orchid, Great Mullein, Henbane, Portland Spurge, Pyramidal Orchid, Scurvygrass, Danish Scurvygrass, Storksbill and Viper's Bugloss.

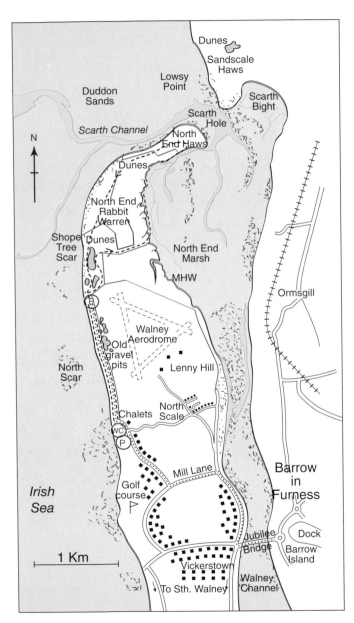

Map: use OS Outdoor Leisure 31, North Pennines, Teesdale and Weardale

WALK 1 ◆ NORTH WALNEY ISLAND

Distance at least 8 km / 5 miles
Time minimum of half a day

LOOK OUT FOR

See flowers listed on previous pages

From Barrow-in-Furness take the A590 across Jubilee Bridge. Immediately over, go R alongside Walney Channel for 900m, then L up Mill Lane for 500m, turning R along West Shore Road to Earnse Point (car park and toilets). Cars can be taken along the shingle track to its end, where you may also park (SD168712). Walk N along continuing track to end of fence on R, then go R into the Nature Reserve. Roam freely on paths (but not on the airfield) and make sure you cross to the salt marshes and explore the dunes and slacks at the northern end of the island. Take a picnic and make a memorable day of it.

A recommended route is shown on the map.

North Walney Island

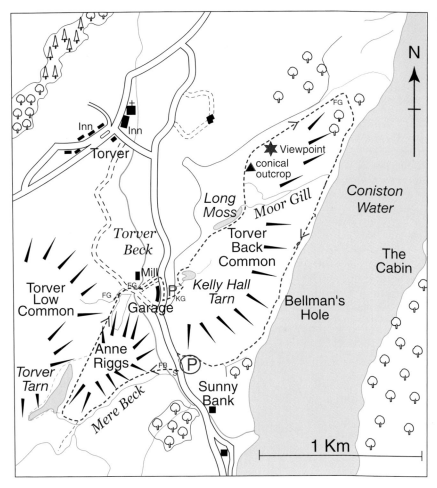

Map: use OS Outdoor Leisure 6, English Lakes, SW

WALK 2
TORVER TARNS & CONISTON WATER

Distance 8 km / 5 miles
Time 2½–3 hours

Take the A5084 between Greenodd and Coniston, and park on the wide verge just N of Sunny Bank Mill (SD 288926). Cross A5084 and take footpath to R of Mere Beck; fork R near top to Torver Tarn. Explore shores. This is common land and access is unrestricted. Then take footpath NNE to Mill Bridge, across which take track L to main road. Turn R for 100m, then opposite garage go L on to Torver Back Common. Explore Kelly Hall Tarn, leaving on an indistinct, boggy path NNE, veering R near top to Long Moss (White Water Lilies). An elevated path by the S side of this tarn reveals its continuation to the L of a conical outcrop, beyond which spectacular views of Coniston Water encourage a picnic stop. The path descends with R forks; keep to the lakeside, which follow R to start.

LOOK OUT FOR

April	Milkmaid, Wood Anemone, Green Alkanet
May	Butterwort, Bogbean, Sanicle
June	Milkwort, Lousewort, Bilberry
July	White Water Lily, Sundew, Water Lobelia
August	Slender St John's Wort, Sneezewort, Redshank
September	Devil's Bit Scabious, Grass of Parnassus
October	Tormentil, Harebell, Mouse-Ear Hawkweed

Birds include Sandpiper, Curlew, Canada and Grey Lag Goose, Pied Wagtail, Raven, Meadow Pipit, Chaffinch, Wren, Blue Tit and Great Tit.

Torver is from the ON *torf*, turf or peat, and ON *erg*, pasture. The early history of the village was pastoral but it grew to house miners who worked the extensive slate quarries on the commons that stretched up the flanks of Coniston Old Man. Slate was led down by cart for export by the now-closed Furness Railway.
Coniston is from OE *cyningestun*, king's manor

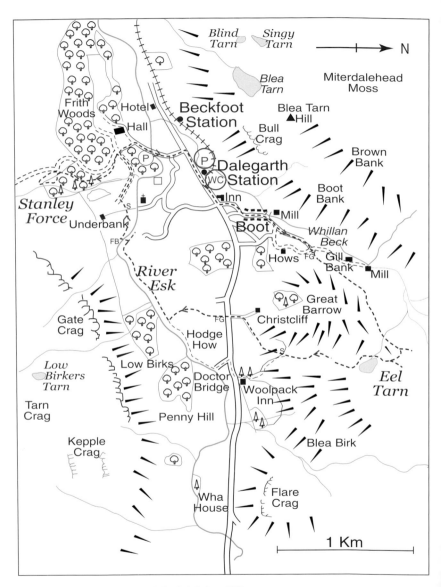

Map: use OS Outdoor Leisure 6, English Lakes, SW

WALK 3
EEL TARN, RIVER ESK & STANLEY FORCE

Distance 9 km / 5½ miles
Time 3–4 hours

Start from Dalegarth Station (NY 173007) on the Hardknott Pass road. Go L along road to Boot, turn L into village. Just before bridge, take a gated lane on R past waterfalls. After 500m, a gate recessed on the R gives access to a path on L, partly walled at first then open. 1.2km on, after a beck crossing, a clearway through the bracken on the R leads to Eel Tarn. Continue round the E of the tarn and start descent towards Woolpack Inn. At a gate and stile on R signed 'Boot or Woolpack Inn', cross stile and follow clear footpath S to a farm approach, turn L and join valley road. Cross straight over to a permitted path leading to the riverside. Go R here, with wall to L until it drops down to a footbridge. Cross bridge and follow path R over Birker Bridge. Continue to bridleway crossing, turn L for 120m, and enter Stanley Ghyll Wood. Explore riverside path up to Stanley Force. Return to the foot of the wood, and follow bridleway to join road over river then main road, where go R back to start.

You can make a day of it by parking at Ravenglass and taking the train.

LOOK OUT FOR

March	Daffodil, Primrose, Celandine, Dog Violet
April	Sweet Cicely, Greater Stitchwort, Pond Water Crowfoot
May	Hedge Parsley, Sorrel, Thyme-leaved Speedwell
June	Cow Wheat, Meadow Vetchling, Butterwort
July	Heath Spotted Orchid, Smooth Hawksbeard, Sundew
August	Felwort, Hemlock Water Dropwort, Lousewort
September	Rat's Tail Plantain, Rest Harrow, Tufted Vetch

You may see or hear Greylag Goose, Mallard, Tufted Duck, Black-headed Gull, Snipe, Buzzard, Raven, Crow, Magpie, Meadow Pipit, Blackbird, Yellowhammer, Skylark, Pied Wagtail, Chaffinch, Great Tit, etc.

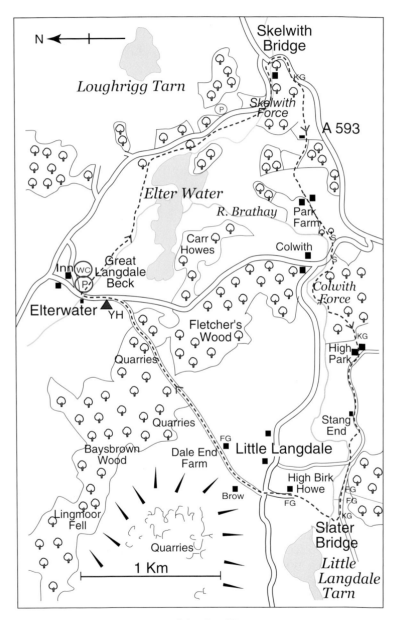

Map: use OS Outdoor Leisure 7, English Lakes, SE

WALK 4
ELTER WATER & LITTLE LANGDALE

Distance 10 km / 6¼ miles
Time 2½–3½ hours

Park in Elterwater National Trust
car park (NY 328047) off the B5343
(Skelwith Bridge–Great Langdale).
Follow streamside path down Langdale
Beck past Elter Water ('Swan Lake')
and Skelwith Force, through slate yard
to A593. Go R along road over bridge
to footpath on R signed Colwith
Bridge, follow to minor road. Here, go
R for a short distance and take footpath
on L for Colwith Force. Continue
along paths to High Park, then along
metalled road past Stang End. At foot
of road go R by beck side to join an old
quarry track, through two gates to a
kissing gate on R leading to Slater
Bridge. Just beyond bridge, riverside
marsh sustains several rare bog plants.
Continue NE past High Birk Howe
Farm to road. Cross road, and pick up
lane slightly L, then follow past Dale
End Farm and Youth Hostel to start.

The name 'force' comes from ON *fors*,
waterfall or rapid. Skelwith comes from
ON *skiallr*, roaring or resounding, Colwith
from ON *kol-vior*, dark forest, or forest where
charcoal was made. The suffix 'with' is from
OE *wipig*, willow, i.e. where willows grow.
Many northern place names date back to
the occupation of the area by Norse settlers
in the ninth century.

LOOK OUT FOR

March	Golden Saxifrage, Primrose, Daffodil
April	Wood Anemone, Dog Violet, Bluebell
May	Globe Flower, Large Bittercress, Cow Wheat
June	Heath Spotted Orchid, Sanicle, Yellow Pimpernel
July	Angelica, Valerian, Yellow Water Lily
August	Bog Asphodel, Lousewort, Bog Lousewort
September	Oxford Ragwort, Toadflax, Sticky Mouse-Ear
October	Spearwort, Red Campion, Marsh Hawksbeard

Birds to see include Buzzard,
Sparrowhawk, Mute Swan,
Mallard, Tufted Duck, Pied
Wagtail, Wren, Robin, Dunnock,
House Sparrow, Chaffinch, Blue
and Great Tits, Robin, Wood
Pigeon, Crow, Magpie, Jay, Greater
Spotted and Green Woodpeckers.

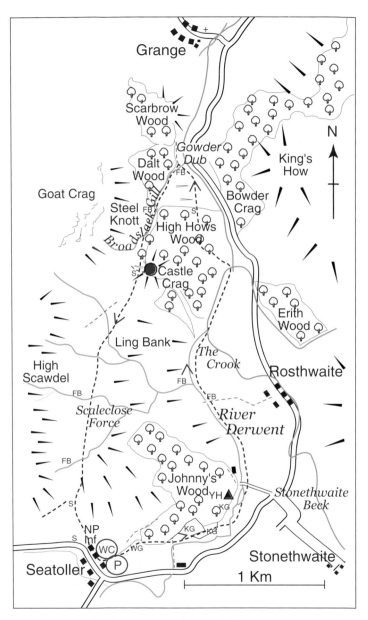

Grange

Scarbrow
Wood

*Gowder
Dub*

Dalt
Wood

FB

King's
How

Goat Crag

Steel
Knott

FB

Bowder
Crag

High Hows
Wood

Broadslack Gill

Castle
Crag

Erith
Wood

Ling Bank

*The
Crook*

High
Scawdel

FB

Rosthwaite

FB

FB

*Scaleclose
Force*

FB

*River
Derwent*

Johnny's
Wood YH

KG

*Stonethwaite
Beck*

S

NP
Inf

KG

KG

WC

WG

P

Seatoller

Stonethwaite

1 Km

Map: use OS Outdoor Leisure 4, English Lakes, NW

WALK 5
RIVER DERWENT & BORROWDALE

Distance 8 km / 5 miles
Time 3–3½ hours

Park in the National Trust car park
at Seatoller (NY 245138), just off the
B5289. Go through the field gate or
stile at NE corner of car park, take
track ahead for 50m then smaller
path to R along wood edge down to
riverside. Proceed, passing in front
of Youth Hostel by riverside path,
eventually ascending a little into High
Hows Wood: note the interesting boggy
flush on R, before returning to riverside
at Gowder Dub. Just before the
footbridge over Broadslack Gill, take
bridleway on L signed Seatoller and
Honister. At a small cairn, a path off
L takes you to the summit of Castle
Crag for panoramic views. Retrace path
back to bridleway and continue towards
Honister Pass. When the pass is in
sight, a kissing gate to L takes you
back down to Seatoller and start.

Borrowdale (from ON *borgordalr*, valley with
a fort) stretches from Seathwaite, reputedly
the wettest place in England with an annual
rainfall of 333cm/131in, to the head of
Derwentwater a little north of Grange, named
from its former importance as the chief farm of
the Furness Abbey monks who owned the dale
in medieval times. Seatoller owes its size, if
not its existence, to the those who laboured in
the Honister slate quarries, worked since 1643.

LOOK OUT FOR

March	Wood Anemone, Pond Water Crowfoot, Celandine
April	Daffodil, Marsh Marigold, Golden Saxifrage
May	Butterwort, Marsh Valerian, New Zealand Willowherb
June	Bog Asphodel, Ragged Robin, Alpine Lady's Mantle
July	Trailing St. John's Wort, Sundew, Heath Spotted Orchid
August	Marsh Thistle, Eyebright, Bog Pimpernel
September	Grass of Parnassus, Red Campion, Yellow Pimpernel
October	Parsley, Hard and Male Ferns, Woodsia

Birds to see and hear include
Wren, Dipper, Willow Warbler,
Wood Warbler, Pied Flycatcher,
Cuckoo, Jackdaw, Crow, Rook,
Grey Wagtail, Pied Wagtail,
Sandpiper, Oyster Catcher, Green
and Greater Spotted Woodpecker,
Chaffinch, Buzzard and many
more.

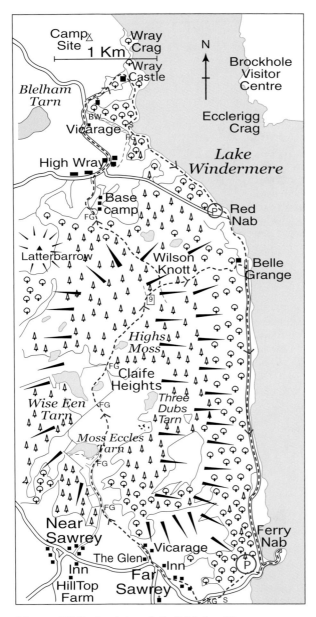

Map: use OS Outdoor Leisure 7, English Lakes, SE

WALK 6 A + B
CLAIFE TARNS & WINDERMERE

Distance A: 10.5 km / 7 miles
or B: 15 km / 9½ miles
Time 4–5½ hours

Park in Bowness at the launch car park (SD 399959) and cross the lake by ferry, or in Scar Wood, one of West's 'stations'* (SD 388955). From the wood follow footpath signed Sawrey and Hill Top, at a sharp bend in road taking footpath on R to Far Sawrey. Continue past hotel to road on R by The Glen and continue along bridleway to Moss Eccles Tarn. A diversion to L round the tarn's south shore is well worth taking. Then from E of tarn continue along bridleway past more tarns to cross a forest road at white post no. 9. Go down through wood to join another grit forest road. For a shorter walk, continue down to Belle Grange and follow lakeside road back to start.

For a wider range of flowers and interest take walk B. From post no. 9 go L along road past Base Camp (National Trust) to High Wray and follow road to Church. Go R past church and Wray Castle, a school for nautical trainees, to lake shore where go R along tracks and road back to start.

* West's Guide Book (1778) identified 'stations' as best viewpoints. This walk goes near Hill Top, Beatrix Potter's first farm, and Wray Castle, which her father rented as a holiday cottage when she was a child.

LOOK OUT FOR

March	Golden Saxifrage, Daffodil, Strawberry
April	Wood Anemone, Marsh Marigold
May	Goldilocks, Comfrey, Marsh Valerian
June	Green Alkanet, Lesser Spearwort, Small Balsam
July	Himalayan Balsam, Feverfew, Claytonia
August	Marsh Woundwort, Bog Pimpernel, Oxford Ragwort
September	Touch-me-not, Welsh Poppy, Hemp-Nettle
October	Sneezewort, Yarrow, Devil's Bit Scabious

Birds include Robin, Coal Tit, Great Tit, Blue Tit, Long-Tailed Tit, Blackbird, Chaffinch, Willow Warbler, Song Thrush, Great Spotted and Green Woodpecker, Buzzard, Pied Flycatcher, Pied Wagtail, Grey Wagtail, Jay, Jackdaw, Rook, Crow, Canada Goose, Wren, Grey Lag Goose, Oyster Catcher, Gulls, Mallard, Coot, Moorhen, Cormorant, Tufted Duck, Goldeneye, Teal and Goosander, among others.

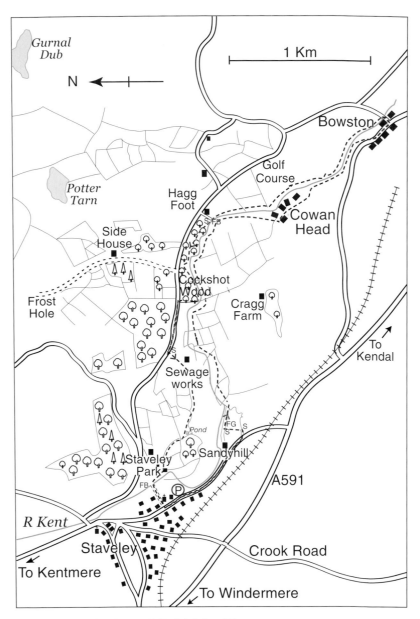

Map: use OS Outdoor Leisure 7, English Lakes, SE

WALK 7
RIVER KENT & COCKSHOT WOOD

Distance 10 km / 6¼ miles
Time 3–4 hours

Park off the A591 in Staveley village (SD 471982). Follow road SE for about 700m to footpath sign on L. Follow through fields then by riverside past former mill at Cowan Head (now holiday apartments) to road at Bowston village. Carry on to road bridge on L, cross, and take riverside footpath on L to Hagg Foot track and bridge. Cross track to stile into Cockshot Wood. Follow woodland path, keeping L at forks, to end of wood. At road go L for 200m, then follow footpath on L past sewage works and Staveley Park Farm to recross river and return to start in Staveley village.

The name Kent, like Kennet, derives from the old British Cunetio, 'from the hills'. The river rises high up in the fells not far from High Street, named after the Roman road that runs along its summit. It flows through Kentmere and Kendal (a corruption of Kentdale) to enter Morecambe Bay near Milnthorpe, once its busy port. Falling over 610m/2,000ft in its 25-mile course, the Kent is the swiftest river in the country; it powered water-mills for grinding corn, fulling cloth, making paper and bobbins, and smelting lead. Only Croppers' paper mill at Burneside still operates; as well as papers and card, it is the sole manufacturer of the red paper used for Remembrance Day poppies.

LOOK OUT FOR

March	Wild Daffodil, Snowdrop, Golden Saxifrage
April	Marsh Marigold, Wood Anemone, Wild Daffodil
May	Pink Purslane, Columbine, Primrose
July	Creeping Bellflower, Fragrant Orchid, Valerian
August	Hemp-Nettle, Monkey Flower, Burnet Saxifrage
September	Yarrow, Marsh Woundwort, Water Mint

Birds to see include Dipper, Pied and Grey Wagtail, Oyster Catcher, Mallard, Tits, Sandpiper, Goosander, Moorhen, Woodcock, Sparrowhawk, Buzzard, Greater Spotted and Green Woodpeckers, Crows.

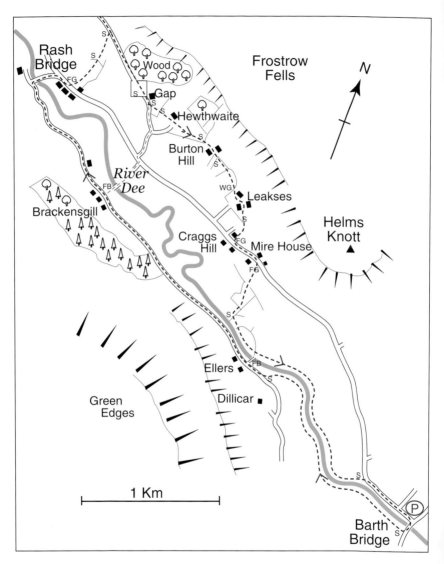

Map: use OS Outdoor Leisure Map 2, Yorkshire Dales West

WALK 8 ◆ DENTDALE

Distance 10.5 km / 6½ miles
Time 3½–4 hours

LOOK OUT FOR

Park on the wide verge just before Barth Bridge, 7km from Sedbergh on the road to Dent (SD 694880). Cross over Barth Bridge and follow footpath (Dales Way) along south bank of River Dee, joining a minor road just before Ellers Farm. Continue along road to Rash Bridge, cross to join valley road, where 160m to R is a footpath on L up over two fields to join a crossing bridleway. Go R along here to Gap Farm, then over fields to Leakses Farm. Descend through fields to Craggs Farm. Go L along road for 250m to footpath on R opposite Mire House to the riverside where a footpath to L leads back to start.

A new footbridge opposite Brackensgill leads to Hewthwaite (a short cut).

April	Goldilocks Buttercup, Town Hall Clock, Butterbur
May	Lady's Mantle, Stitchwort, Thyme-leaved Speedwell
June	Smooth Hawksbeard, Meadow Vetchling, Yellow Rattle
July	Welsh Poppy, Meadow Cranesbill, Bush Vetch
August	Nipplewort, Knotgrass, Sticky Mouse-Ear
September	Oxford Ragwort, Woody Nightshade, Hedge Woundwort

Dentdale is the valley of the River Dee, which rises on the flanks of Whernside and flows NW to join the River Rawthay to the south of Sedbergh whence, after a short distance, it joins the River Lune to go south through Kirkby Lonsdale and Lancaster into Morecambe Bay. The whole district is strong in Quaker history, George Fox having founded The Religious Order of Friends on Firbank Fell near Sedbergh in 1652. The Friends' Meeting House at Brigg Flatts (1675), the oldest meeting house in northern England, is well worth a visit, and a very cordial welcome is given to all visitors. Dent Parsonage was the home of Adam Sedgwick (1785–1873), Woodwardian Professor at the University of Cambridge, sometimes called 'the father of English geology' because of his discovery of the Cambrian system.

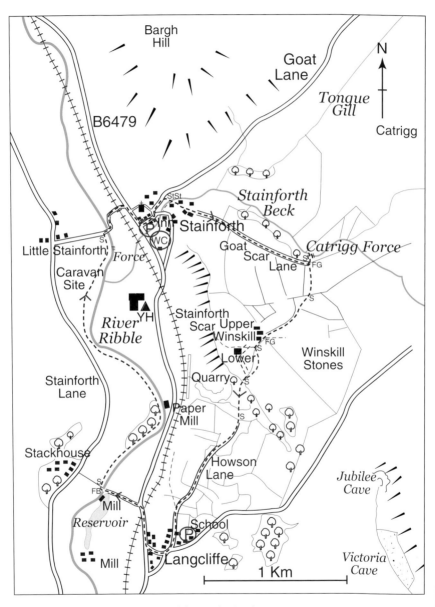

Map: use OS Outdoor Leisure 10, Yorkshire Dales South
or OS Outdoor Leisure 2, Yorkshire Dales West

WALK 9
RIVER RIBBLE & CATRIGG FORCE

Distance 7 km / 4¹/₂ miles
Time 2¹/₂–3¹/₂ hours

Park in Langcliffe car park alongside school (SD 8236511). Take rough track to W of car park, turning R at tarmac lane past the war memorial to main road where turn R. After crossing railway, go over road and take lane on L down to river. Cross footbridge then follow riverside path past Stainforth Falls to bridge. Cross and ascend up lane to main road. Go R, and cross to 2nd L (car park and toilets). Continue along road into village bearing L at T-junction then across green and stepping stones (if impassable, take alternative streamside path from village opposite pub) to a steep, stony track, Goat Scar Lane. At the lane head a stile to L leads down to the 18m/60ft Catrigg Force. After exploration return to the stile and take a farm track past Upper and Lower Winskill. Go through a gate signed Langcliffe, then take footpath on L over a stile. This leads to Howson Lane, Langcliffe village and start.

LOOK OUT FOR

April	Coltsfoot, Sorrel, Marsh Marigold
May	Greater Stitchwort, Primrose, Bluebell
June	Meadow Saxifrage, Hairy Rockcress, Rough Hawkbit
July	Rest Harrow, Field Scabious, Comfrey
August	Broad-leaved Willowherb, Welsh Poppy, Shepherd's Purse
September	Devil's Bit Scabious, Smooth Hawksbeard, Meadow Buttercup

Birds to see include Grey Heron, Canada Goose, Mallard, Goosander, Moorhen, Oyster Catcher, Snipe, Pied, Grey and Yellow Wagtails, Wren, Great Spotted Woodpecker, Skylark, Wheatear, Willow Warbler, Chaffinch, Blue Tit, Great Tit, Nuthatch, etc.

Stainforth, stony ford
Langcliffe, long cliff (limestone escarpment)
Stainforth Force is renowned for large salmon leaping up the waterfalls as they make their way upriver to spawning grounds. Possibly the most spectacular displays occur in October.

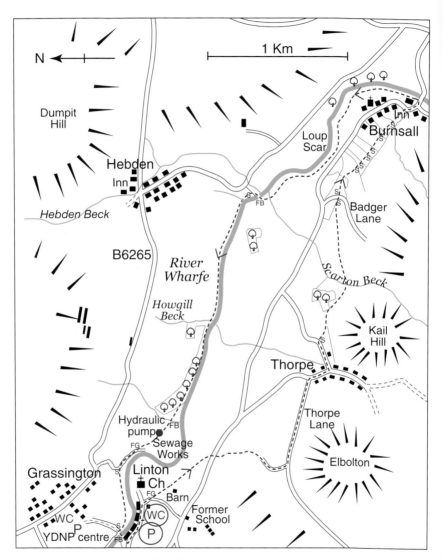

Map: use OS Outdoor Leisure 10, Yorkshire Dales South

WALK 10
MID WHARFEDALE & BURNSALL

Distance 11 km / 7 miles
3¹/₂–4¹/₂ hours

Park at Yorkshire Dales National Park car park near Linton Church (SE 002632). Go R along road; 100m past toilets take walled lane on R, then footpath heading SE, L of barn over fields to Burnsall Road. Across road take footpath S to join walled lane leading to Thorpe Lane. Turn L to Thorpe hamlet. At triangular green go L for 300m, then take footpath on R over stile through meadows to Burnsall (toilets, cafés, inn). Join Dales Way footpath E of inn and follow river past Loup Scar, across Hebden Suspension Bridge and on to Sedber Lane. Go L over bridge to road, then L to car park.

Sedber Lane, Grassington, leads to the Yorkshire Dales National Park Information Centre where toilets, useful literature, maps and information are available. The walk could start from here.

LOOK OUT FOR

April	Goldilocks, Creeping Buttercup, Marsh Marigold
May	Meadow Saxifrage, Hairy Rockcress, Mouse-Ear
June	Watercress, Sticky Mouse-Ear, Wintercress
July	Marsh Helleborine, Meadow Vetchling, Vetch
August	Marjoram, Monkey Flower, Water Mint
September	Apple Mint, Groundsel, Field Scabious

Just before the sewage works there is a hydraulic water pump close to the path (see map). Between the pump and the path is a boggy area that supports many rarer plants such as Marsh Helleborine, Fool's Watercress, Bird's Eye Primrose, Butterwort, Small Scabious, Grass of Parnassus, Rock Rose and Creeping Cinquefoil.

Grassington from OE *gresing*, grazing farm
Burnsall from OE *Brynis halh*, secret corner of Bryni
Thorpe, OE, a minor settlement or farm
Hebden from OE, hip (fruit) valley
Linton, from OE *lin-tun*, flax settlement
Wharfe from OBrit *weorpan*, twisting river

Goosanders and nesting Sandmartins will be the most obvious birds, but keen eyes will also spot Kingfishers, Sandpipers and Dippers.

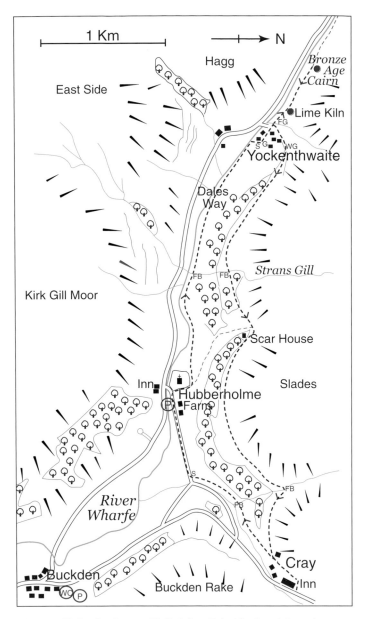

Map: use OS Outdoor Leisure 30, Yorkshire Dales North and Central

WALK 11 A + B
UPPER WHARFE & HUBBERHOLME

Distance A: 12 km / 7½ miles
or B: 8 km / 5 miles
Time A: 3½–4½ hours
or B: 3 hours

Park at Hubberholme riverside near the church (SD 926783). Go through field gate between the farm and the church and soon fork L to follow the Dales Way by riverside to Yockenthwaite. (Continue for 600m to view lime kiln and Bronze Age burial cairn. Return to Yockenthwaite). Take track behind farm buildings to footpath on R that leads to a limestone terrace above Scar Woods. To shorten walk, at Scar House go down track to church, but preferably continue on contour to Cray (inn). From inn retrace path 200m to follow footpath on L down Cray Gill to road, where go R back to start.

LOOK OUT FOR

April	Toothwort, Town Hall Clock, Marsh Marigold
May	Kidney Vetch, Greater Stitchwort, Meadow Buttercup
June	Watercress, Red Campion, Welsh Poppy
July	Marjoram, Fragrant Orchid, Spotted Orchid
August	Good King Henry, Meadow Vetchling, Marsh Hawksbeard
September	Groundsel, Spearmint, Pineapple Mayweed

Birds to see include Curlew, Oyster Catcher, Sandpiper, Goosander, Mallard, Pied Wagtail, Dipper, Buzzard, Kestrel, Carrion Crow, Jackdaw, Lapwing, Wren, Willow Warbler, Swallow, House Martin, Sand Martin, Chaffinch, Meadow Pipit, etc.

Hubberholme (pronounced Ubberam) means the settlement of Hunburg (unusually, a Norse woman's name)

Yockenthwaite means the woodland clearing of Eogan, an Old Irish name

Cray, fresh or clean, from OBrit *crei*

The Church of St Michael and All Angels, once a forest chapel, has a unique 1558 rood loft; the ashes of the writer J. B. Priestley are scattered in the churchyard.

The Bronze Age burial cairn commemorates a former chieftain who was buried here. Near to it is a traditional lime kiln in which local limestone was roasted then slaked to sweeten the soil of the surrounding hay meadows.

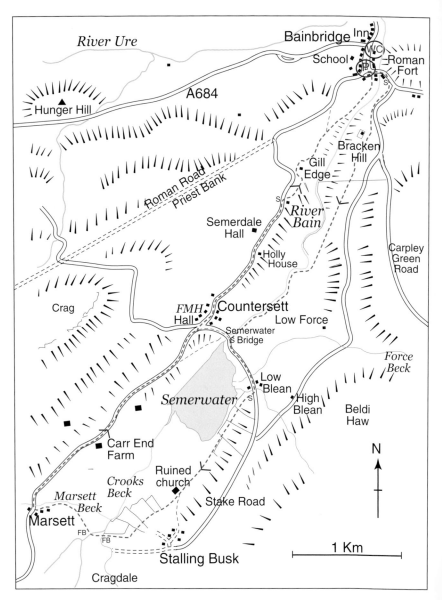

Map: use OS Outdoor Leisure 30, Yorkshire Dales North and Central

WALK 12 ◆ RIVER BAIN & SEMERWATER

Distance 13 km / 8 miles
Time 4–5 hours

Park alongside village green in Bainbridge (SD 934902). Walk S along A684 over bridge to footpath on R. Ascend Bracken Hill and continue by riverside to Semerwater Bridge. Go L along shore on road past Low Blean to footpath on right. Along here pass Semerwater and ruined church. Just past church fork R to Marsett. Turn R along road to Countersett, past Friends' Meeting House (visitors welcome) and Smardale Hall to footpath on R. Field path veers behind Gill Edge and continues NE. At a fork go R to flank riverside wood and return to Bainbridge.

LOOK OUT FOR

April	Coltsfoot, Marsh Marigold, Bush Vetch
May	Town Hall Clock, Milkmaid, Marsh Valerian
June	Dame's Violet, Forget-me-not, Ragged Robin
July	Yarrow, Sow-Thistle, Yellow Rattle
August	Yellow Water Lily, Meadow Vetchling, Lady's Mantle
September	Feverfew, Red Campion, Bush Vetch

Birds to be seen include Mallard, Oyster Catcher, Curlew, Redshank, Sandpiper, Lapwing, Pied, Grey and Yellow Wagtails, Moorhen, Mute Swan, Wigeon, Tufted Duck, Tits, Chaffinch, Swallow, House Martin, Buzzard and Wren.

Bain means straight, from ON *beinn*. At only 4 km/2½ miles long, the Bain, which drains Semerwater into the River Ure, is England's shortest river. Brough Hill in Bainbridge is capped by a Roman fort dating from 80 AD. Bainbridge, once on the edge of a hunting forest, continues the tradition of a hornblower who warns people to leave the forest at impending nightfall.

Semerwater is a tautological indicator of its past occupiers: OE *sae*, OE *mere*, and OE *water* all mean the same thing.

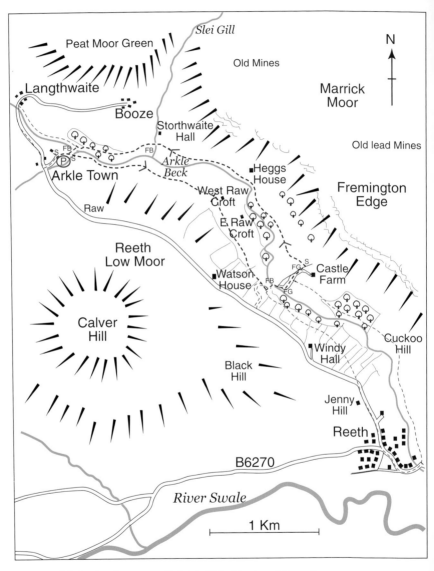

Map: use OS Outdoor Leisure 30, Yorkshire Dales North and Central

WALK 13 ◆ ARKLE BECK, SWALEDALE

Distance 6.5 km / 4 miles
Time 2½–3 hours

LOOK OUT FOR

Park in Arkle Town, 5 km NW of
Reeth (NZ 008020). At end of hamlet
take footpath across disused churchyard
to riverside. At footbridge keep to
W side of Arkle Beck and proceed
downstream through fields past Raw
Croft Farms to track over bridge.
Follow track through field gate nearly
to Castle Farmhouse then take footpath
on L (yellow circles) to descend to
riverside path. Cross footbridge over
Slei Gill and on to footbridge below
Arkle Town. Cross and return to start.

April	Coltsfoot, Marsh Marigold, Forget-me-not
May	Ground Elder, Spring Sandwort, Sorrel
June	Welsh Poppy, Greater Stitchwort, Kidney Vetch
July	Meadow and Creeping Buttercups, Hogweed, Feverfew
August	Hedge Woundwort, Monkey Flower, Chickweed
September	White Clover, Bush Vetch, Yarrow

Typical birds include Curlew,
Oyster Catcher, Sandpiper,
Goosander, Mallard, Robin, Pied
Wagtail, Chaffinch, Meadow Pipit,
Blackbird, Song Thrush, Willow
Warbler, Wheatear, Swallow,
House Martin, Skylark and
Buzzard.

This area was once famous for the mining and
smelting of lead and silver. Apart from the
ruins of ancillary buildings and spoil heaps
('tailings'), a feature of the former industry
is shown by 'hushes'. The old lead miners
prospected for lead veins by damming water
courses high up on the hillsides until a
substantial volume of water had accumulated.
Then the dam was breached, the water came
'hushing' down, scouring loose soil and rock
from its course to reveal any lead veins which
could then be exploited.
Arkengarthdale means valley of the garth
(enclosure) of the Viking chief Arkil.

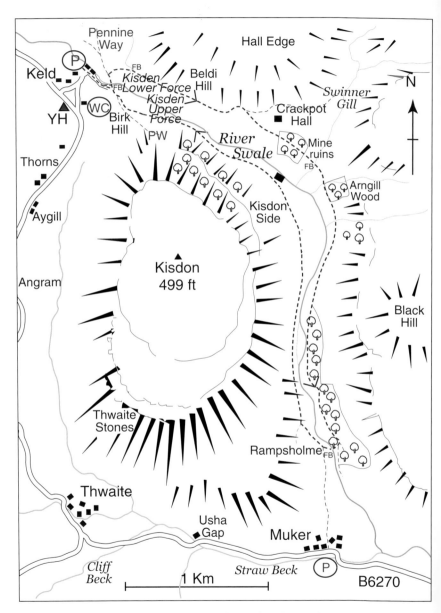

Map: use OS Outdoor Leisure 30, Yorkshire Dales North and Central

WALK 14 ◆ UPPER SWALEDALE & KELD

Distance 9 km / 6 miles
Time 3–3½ hours

Park in Keld village car park
(NY 893013). Follow lane SE, going
L at fork down to river. Across bridge
take bridleway to R past Beldi Hill,
below Crackpot Hall, over Swinner
Gill and by riverside to Rampsholme
footbridge. Cross, and follow footpath
to R through riverside meadows and
woods back to start.

Keld means spring (ON *kelda*, Dan *kaelde*),
an element seen in the Lancastrian and
Cumbrian names Kellet, Kelswick and
Threlkeld. Keld was once known as
Applctreekeld.
Muker, narrow field, from ON *mior*, narrow,
and ON *akr*, field
Swale, whirling, rushing river, from OE *swillan*

As in Walk 13, the remains of the district's
lead mining past are everywhere in evidence,
especially round Swinnergill. Many of the
ruined buildings were the homesteads of lead
miners who for the sake of their health often
worked only 3–4 days a week underground and
the remainder farming in the open air. They
erected the buildings themselves from locally
quarried stone.

This walk coincides for part of its route with
two long-distance footpaths, the Pennine Way
and the Coast-to-Coast Walk.

LOOK OUT FOR

April	Coltsfoot, Goldilocks Buttercup, Town Hall Clock
May	Marsh Marigold, Primrose, Spring Sandwort
June	Meadow Saxifrage, Lady's Mantle, Bush Vetch
July	Forget-me-not, Monkey Flower, Sticky Mouse-Ear
August	Great Bindweed, Nipplewort, Meadow Vetchling
September	Water Mint, Shepherd's Purse, Yarrow

Birds include Dipper, Wagtails,
Mallard, Meadow Pipit, Swallow,
House Martin, Chaffinch, Tits,
Rook, Crow, Raven, Magpie,
Buzzard, etc.

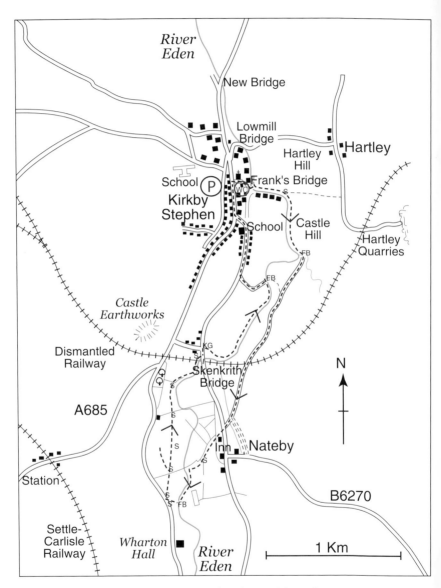

Map: use OS Outdoor Leisure 19, Howgill Fells and Upper Eden Valley

WALK 15
RIVER EDEN & KIRKBY STEPHEN

Distance 7 km / 4½ miles
Time 2½–3½ hours

Park in Kirkby Stephen village (SD 775087). Take road in front of church to Frank's Bridge, cross, and take riverside path R which veers R after kissing gate and eventually becomes a walled lane. At fork beside stream go R towards Nateby. Follow bridleway across road to a footbridge over River Eden up to Wharton Hall drive, then take footpath on R across fields to Skenkrith Force (good picnic place on rocks). Go L along road for 100m, then follow riverside footpath on R through Skenkrith Park (look out for contemporary sculptures) to join a walled lane on L, opposite a footbridge, to return to the start.

Alternatively, cross footbridge to meet outward path and turn L back to start (this adds little to the overall distance).

LOOK OUT FOR

April	Goldilocks Buttercup, Town Hall Clock, Toothwort
May	Lady's Mantle, Red Campion, Meadow Saxifrage
June	White Clover, Hairy Rockcress, Good King Henry
July	Feverfew, Ground Elder, Marsh Hawksbeard
August	Broad-leaved Willowherb, Rest Harrow, Comfrey
September	Great Willowherb, Nipplewort, Yarrow

Birds that may be seen include Goosander, Mallard, Dipper, Pied Wagtail, Coot, Moorhen, Swallow, House Martin, Chaffinch, Cuckoo, Chiffchaff, Willow Warbler, Oyster Catcher, Curlew, Blackbird, Song Thrush, Wren, Buzzard and Parakeets (locally owned but flying free!).

Kirkby Stephen means a settlement with St Stephen's church; OE *by* indicating a former Danish settlement. It was once an important market town that specialised in woollen stockings. Wharton Hall, seat of Lord Wharton, was built in the fourteenth century and expanded in the sixteenth.

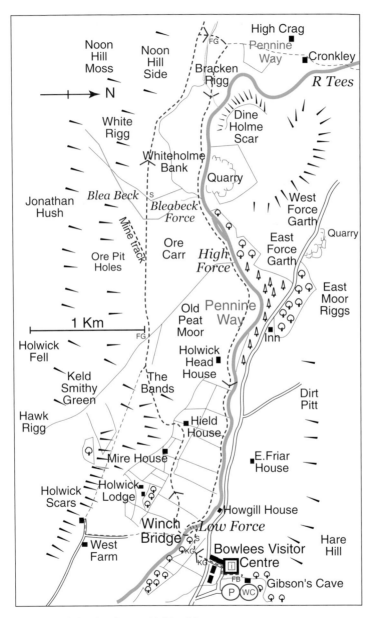

Map: use OS Outdoor Leisure 31, Teesdale

WALK 16 ◆ RIVER TEES & HIGH FORCE

**Distance 12 km / 7½ miles
Time 4–5 hours**

Park at Durham Wildlife Trust's car
park at Bowlees (NY 908284). Pass
Information Centre to cross road down
to Winch Bridge. Explore surroundings
for many rare flowers. Cross suspension
bridge and follow path slightly L then,
after 40m, footpath on R skirting Mire
House that joins a farm track. Go R.
Just short of Hield House the footpath
veers L at a wall corner past a field
barn, and angles indistinctly SW up
The Bands to join a bridleway, an
old miners' track. Follow to R. 600m
beyond a gate and a National Nature
Reserve signboard, take a footpath
forking to R. After two stream
crossings, at 2 mile stones, go R for
300m to join Pennine Way path. Go R
here to High Force then Winch Bridge.
Cross to return to start.

Part of this walk is along the Pennine Way:
High Force is 146 miles from the start at Edale
in Derbyshire, and 124 miles from the end
at Kirk Yetholm, just north of the border in
Scotland.
Industrial remains of lead mining abound in
upper Teesdale.

LOOK OUT FOR

April	Marsh Marigold, Wood Anemone, Water Avens
May	Cow Parsley, Good King Henry, Early Purple Orchid
June	Monkey Flower, Vetch, Globe Flower, Yellow Rattle
July	Meadow Vetchling; Butterfly, Fragrant, Northern Marsh and Heath Spotted Orchids
August	Hedge Woundwort, Kidney Vetch, Sneezewort
September	Felwort, Golden Rod, Devil's Bit Scabious

Birds to see include Sandpiper,
Dipper, Sand Martin, Swallow,
House Martin, Yellow, Grey and
Pied Wagtails, Oyster Catcher,
Curlew, Golden Plover, Spotted
and Pied Flycatcher, Nuthatch,
Treecreeper, Finches, Wheatear,
Snipe, Skylark, Meadow Pipit,
Buzzard, Red Grouse.

FURTHER READING

Back, P., *The Illustrated Herbal* (Hamlyn, 1987)

Blamey, M. and C. Grey-Wilson, *Illustrated Flora of Britain and Northern Europe* (Hodder & Stoughton, 1994)

Blunt, W., *The Complete Naturalist*, (Collins, 1971)

Bown, D., *RHS Encyclopaedia of Herbs* (Dorling Kindersely, 1995)

Ceres, *The Healing Power of Herbal Teas* (Thorsons, 1984)

Chevallier, A., *Encyclopaedia of Medicinal Plants* (Dorling Kindersley, 1996)

Coombes, A. J., *Dictionary of Plant Names* (Collingridge, 1985)

Culpeper, N., *Culpeper's Complete Herbal* (1699; reprint Wordsworth, 1995))

de Gex., J., *A Medieval Herbal* (Pavilion, 1995)

Dorfler, H. P. and G. Roselt, *Dictionary of Healing Plants* (Blandford, 1989)

Duncan, J. E. and R. W. Robson, *Pennine Flowers* (Dalesman, 1977)

Clapham, A. R., ed., *Upper Teesdale* (Collins, 1978)

Fitter, R. A. and M. Blamey, *Wild Flowers of Britain and Northern Europe* (Collins, 1974)

Gerard, J., *Gerard's Herbal* (reprint Senate, 1994)

Gilmour, J. and M. Walters, *Wild Flowers* (Collins New Naturalist Series, 1954)

Gledhill, D., *The Names of Plants* (Cambridge University Press, 2002)

Gordon, L., *A Country Herbal* (Webb & Bowes, 1980)

Grieve, M., *A Modern Herbal* (Tiger, 1931)

Grigson, G., *The Englishman's Flora* (Phoenix House, 1958)

Grigson, G., *Dictionary of English Plant Names* (Lane, 1973)

Grounds, R., *Ferns* (Readers' Union, 1975)

Halliday, G, *A Flora of Cumbria* (Lancaster University, 1997)

Launert, E., *Edible Medicinal Plants of Britain and Northern Europe* (Country Life, 1981)

Louseley, J. E., *Wild Flowers of Chalk and Limestone* (Collins New Naturalist Series, 1950)

Mabey, R., *Flora Britannica* (Sinclair Stevenson, 1996)

McClintock, D. and R. S. R. Fitter, *Pocket Guide to Wild Flowers* (Collins, 1956)

Grieve, M., *A Modern Herbal* (Cape, 1931)

Merryweather, J. and M. Hill, *The Fern Guide* (Field Studies Council, 1992)

Millward, D., *A Flora of Wensleydale* (Yoredale Nature Society, 1988)

Phillips, R., *Wild Flowers of Britain* (Ward Lock, 1977)

Press, B., *Green Guide: Herbs* (New Holland, 1994)

Raistrick, A. and J. L. Illingworth, *The Face of N.W. Yorkshire* (Dalesman, 1949)

Raven, J. and M. Walters, *Mountain Flowers* (Collins New Naturalist Series, 1956)

Sanecki, K. N., *Complete Book of Herbs* (Macdonald, 1974)

Stearn, W. T., *Botanical Latin* (David & Charles, 1966)

Summerhayes, V. S., *Wild Orchids of Britain* (Collins New Naturalist Series, 1951)

Vickery, R., *A Dictionary of Plant Lore* (Oxford University Press, 1995)

Watts, W. M., *A School Flora* (Longmans, 1905)

INDEX OF PLANT NAMES

This index covers plants in the Directory and the Walks of this volume. Botanical names are given, in parentheses, for Directory plants only.